Dedicated to the memory of dear friends,
Douglas Lord, Gael McRae,
Leroy Wells and Corty Cammann.

TABLE OF CONTENTS

INTRODUCTION

As a young man, I wondered what life was like during the Renaissance. That era seemed so vibrant. Outmoded traditions collapsed. New vistas emerged. People developed fresh dreams. Dying embers sparked refining fires. Decaying political structures slipped into history's archives. Reality became grounded in the substantial, and humanity's intellectual powers exploded. However, this shift took a long time, for communal rebirthing of this magnitude requires generations to gestate.

I now realize we know a lot about reconstructing society, for we are partway through an equally monumental period. Renewal on this scale is both taxing and exciting. Nations vibrate with fresh growing pains. New complexities stimulate nostalgia for simpler days. Global wealth and the numbers locked in impoverished contexts grow exponentially. Despair and hope spawn poison arrows and skyrocketing aspirations, so each step has to be taken with cautious courage.

Something special has been occurring since a young Albert Einstein[1] penned on a piece of paper $E = mc^2$. A century later, we are discovering how to "hold Infinity in the palm of the hand and Eternity in an hour."[2] Some tentative shapes of this epoch have begun to emerge, as concepts like quantum, ecological thinking, collective consciousness, synchronicity, holograms, fractals, nanotechnology, strange attractors, and DNA have entered everyday language.

The future is full of unknowns. It has already acquired a life of its own, which may cause us to rise or fall. How we handle the tumult will determine if this is a new dawn or an elongated darkness.

i

Although we are shaping and being shaped by these transitions, we may never know the impact of our actions. Posterity will decipher what resulted from our fortitude and our oversight, our longings and our patience.

Many new intellectual and societal pillars are currently being built into the foundation of our shared lives. This book focuses on just one, that *all of life is predicated on abundance.*

This assertion is made even though the global world order is being built on an economic system that is based on scarcity. It seems inconceivable that scarcity could be an adequate scaffold to support such complexity. Presently, money can be made only when there is genuine or artificially induced scarcity. For example, when water was freely available, it was assigned no economic value, but as streams got polluted, it became easy to sell water. As we grew afraid of the liquid gushing out of urban faucets, many of us began to buy bottled water, even though it often has as many impurities and tastes no better than what a municipality supplies.[3] Also, a liter of water in a plastic container costs more than the equivalent amount of fuel that has to be extracted from the earth and refined!

It is time to build a form of economics centered on abundance. Because almost everything rests on the established monetary system, this will have to be implemented gradually, however, for chaos would reign if the present financial structures were suddenly discarded and replaced.

Before we can create the new economics, we need to collectively understand what abundance means. Since humanity has the scarcity paradigm well internalized, I propose that we begin by practicing the art of describing everyday events using the abundance paradigm instead of over-chronicling our misfortunes. This book is a starting point in this reconstruction process.

RENEWAL

It is springtime. As buds burst into bloom and birds rehearse the season's symphony, humanity awakens again to new possibilities. With nature's rebirthings, we are reminded that *the world is an abundant place.* Everything we truly need is available to us now, if we can access it.

We live in a world of abundance! I wish I could believe that. An inner voice protests. "Open your eyes! Look at the hungry children, breadwinners losing their jobs, long lines of refugees fleeing famine, broken economic systems, and political oppression. Scarcity is everywhere. Where is the abundance?" Another voice replies, "We are bombarded so often by images of scarcity the bountifulness surrounding us is all but impossible to recognize."

Like breathing, abundance is so close we tend to overlook it. For example, at day's end, we are presented with nature's most restorative gift, sleep. Even if we lie awake longing for more joy, more resilience, more anything, such images of the plentiful indicate that our sense of abundance is just below the surface. Then there are moments when its power is unmistakable, looking at vistas from a mountaintop, holding a newborn, watching the sun depart so other places can be warmed as we get the requisite respite from its everlasting intensity.

Although images of abundance fade during fallow times, they resurface when the over- and under-resourced claim our common destiny or when adversaries become allies. Even when there are shortages, we are sustained by a biology based on nature's lavishness. Also, we have minds that can participate in knowledge creation, can discern what we don't know, can recall the beauty of yesterdays' sunsets, and anticipate tomorrows' sunrises. "In the depth of winter, I finally learned that there was in me an invincible summer," said Camus on behalf of us all.[4]

It is our *belief in possibility* that makes possibility possible.

"Tread carefully when it comes to beliefs, privilege reality!" This thought is always with me. As a person who reveres the verifiable, I have no desire to heed the distorted sounds reverberating in the hollow echo chambers of the mind. Every part of me wants to be connected to the essential. However, a part of me also recognizes that our collective belief in scarcity contributes to the very scarcity we wish to banish.

I came to recognize the presence of abundance during the early days of the HIV/AIDS crisis. This was a strange context to make such a discovery because everything about that devastating era oozed scarcity. We became aware of AIDS in the 1980s when people were dying from a completely unknown disease. What an awful dose of scarcity, death, and zero knowledge of its cause! No one knew how it was transmitted, and there was no cure! Many feared it was carried by insects or was seeping out of buildings' heating and cooling ducts. When we realized that people were dying due to the malnutrition caused by HIV/AIDS, a small group of us started a nonprofit, Metropolitan AIDS Neighborhood Nutrition Alliance (MANNA). Our goal was to ensure that every person in Philadelphia living with HIV had the right, tailor-made nutritional support needed to sustain them during their decline. This was our way of expressing concern for our community members who were being shunned by society.

I served as chair of MANNA's board for the first several years and wrote a book about our experiences.[5] It was subtitled *Ten ⁓ⁿˢ in Abundance*. Here is a sample of the findings that stunned ⅃ us: whenever we were lost, someone appeared to show us the way; the greatest insights came from the most vulnerable in our midst; MANNA's strengths were its vulnerabilities, and its vulnerabilities were its strengths; love grows when given away; the miraculous is contained within the mundane.

WHAT IS ABUNDANCE?

Abundance is a way of seeing, a method of thinking, a form of emoting and a manner of intuiting. So is scarcity, which thrives when abundance is impeded. Abundance and scarcity exist in nature. They also apply to human happenings. We tend to think of scarcity as shortages and abundance as being awash in excesses. These notions are reconceptualized in this book.

While things may be deemed scarce or abundant, neither is an absolute. Both scarcity and abundance vary along continua. Sometimes an extreme amount of each is used to anchor a scale's end. That works for something quantifiable, like a harvest that falls somewhere between dreadful and great, where both are treated as opposites. Another perspective is that, although they may appear to be antithetical, each is present within the other. In this sense they are parts of a duo as with *yes* and *no,* or *light* and *dark.* If we have never experienced the dark, we would always be in the light but never know we are in the light. Or if we are only ever in the dark, we could not imagine light. We would be enshrined in darkness but not be aware of it.[6] Likewise, without scarcity, it would not be possible to construct the concept of abundance, and vice versa.

Since we generally know what we lack, scarcity is easy to identify. However, abundance is more complex. Often, the less we need, the larger the proportion of our necessities that can be met. Or those wanting to be more informed, more influential, or more anything come to discover that as with pruning a garden, limits can facilitate growth. Also, too much abundance, too many options, can be as problematic as few possibilities, for unbounded systems can easily become either excessively expansive or overly constricted!

Scarcity is established by examining the relationship between what exists and what we think we need.[7] This is concrete and easy to verify. Using similar thinking, having more than enough would be deemed as a definition of abundance. However, a more important form of bountifulness is the *untapped possibility waiting to be activated.* This kind of abundance moves the emphasis from the existent to the emergent. But it is difficult to assess because it involves accessing the unseen, imagining what could be, or releasing what has yet to become manifest.

Peter Diamandis and Steven Kotler, in their book titled *Abundance,*[8] offer a classic image of scarcity. It is a person having to scrape just to survive. They do not imply that abundance is basking in excess. Their definition of abundance is having "a life predicated on *doing things that are fulfilling and inwardly meaningful*" (emphasis mine). Abundance involves balancing consumption and replenishment, decay and regeneration, expired pasts and future dreams. This view of abundance also recognizes the value of restrictions. Like a pregnancy approaching full term, scarcity shows the virtue of moving beyond a confining space and entering a landscape of what is to be.

I will illustrate the everyday meanings of abundance and scarcity by drawing upon the thoughts formulated by Diamandis and Kotler plus Sendhil Mullainathan and Eldar Shafir's text, titled *Scarcity.*[9] *Abundance* presents a logic based on innovations in science and technology developed by the Kurzweil Singularity community. It is awash with sociotechnical nuggets. Behavioral economists who drew on social psychology and sociology wrote *Scarcity*.

I will first discuss the *Abundance* book that reports on two of humanity's major challenges, *water* and *energy*, both of which are integral to environmental viability. Second, I will address *Scarcity*, a psycho-philosophical approach to this concept at the heart of economics. I use these two texts as both a starting platform and as a point of departure.

WATER AND ENERGY

Water is essential for all living creatures. Eco-disasters result from too much or too little of it, floods, forest fires, droughts, or blizzards! In 2000, a billion people did not have access to clean drinking water and 2 billion were without adequate sanitation systems.[10] While there is ample water on our planet, 97.5 percent of it is in the oceans, 2 percent is in the polar ice caps, and 0.5 percent is on land.[11] The issue is not lack of water but its saltiness and location. Demands on earth's water exceed supply, given our priorities. For example, 100 gallons of water are consumed producing a single egg, or one watermelon, or a flagon of wine. Beef sufficient for a family meal requires 2,500 gallons. The bottled-water industry annually draws 10 billion gallons from aquifers that took nature thousands of years to fill.[12] The rural sector is impacted the most. Eighty-five percent of people with insufficient clean drinking water live on farms, and 2 million children living in rural areas die each year due to dirty water.[13]

However, technologies already exist that can correct this water imbalance. These three breakthroughs illustrate how this problem is being addressed. First, a filtration system with a one-nanometer aperture (i.e., a billionth of a meter) has been invented, which can filter out bacteria, salt, parasites, viruses, and arsenic. This makes possible desalination, requiring minimal energy.[14] Second, several nanotech innovations are changing the water landscape, such as self-cleaning plumbing devices that prevent corrosion and automatically repair pipes, along with a thin layer of nano-based hydrophobic sand under desert topsoil, which can reduce water losses by 75 percent. Also, modern refrigerators are reducing by 50 percent the loss of fresh produce, are removing inefficiencies in the food supply chain, and are shrinking water usage by 35 percent per person.[15] Third is the change in sanitation, with high-tech toilets able to cremate feces, evaporate urine, sterilize bodily secretions, and convert biowaste into chemicals, fertilizer, and energy.[16]

These changes require new energy systems. For decades, each person has used at least a couple of kilowatt-hours per day to deal with just the basics. Multiply this by the world's population and combine it with what is used by business, transportation, public works, etc.—the amount of natural resources needed to sustain the world is gigantic.[17] However, humanity has come a long way. This is obvious if we calculate the hours of work it takes to acquire something.[18] Thirty-five hundred years ago in the oil lantern era, an hour of lighting cost 50 hours of labor. The equivalent is now about a second of a worker's wage, a 100,000-fold savings. A stagecoach trip in the 19th century took two weeks and a month's wages. That trip is now done by plane in two hours, with the cost being one day of a middle-incomer's earnings.[19] Yet there are still 1.5 billion people without access to electricity, making it very hard for them to get clean water, an essential for maintaining health. Energy, water, poverty, and health are mutually reinforcing. To resolve such problems, the interdependencies among them have to be addressed.[20]

We know that solar energy is the answer to so many difficulties, because it is plentiful and does not deplete anything. The energy reaching the North African deserts alone is 40 times the world's current electricity supply.[21] In a single hour, more energy from sunlight lands on the earth than a year's supply of fossil fuel. That is 8,000 times what is needed to run the world in its current condition and several hundred times what is required to sustain 10 billion people. Solar technology is also scalable. If its use increases at current rates, 100 percent penetration will be reached in the 2030s, and by 2050, humanity will have 10 times the amount of energy we need.[22] Even if only a fraction of this is realized, the possibilities are astonishing.

Establishing efficient ways to distribute energy has been hard but that is changing. Using the WWW as a model, the Enernet is set up to function as a smart grid facilitating the exchange of power between multiple producers and consumers. As with logging on and off the Internet, the Enernet can receive and store energy and data about power in many places, cars, factories, appliances, etc., at all points along the energy production-distribution-consumption supply chain. However, this is a holographic rather than a chain structure.[23] The Internet has a few billion devices with IP addresses, but the Enernet's interconnections are much larger.[24]

Solar energy tied to desalination will help greatly, as large amounts of low-cost energy propel filtration systems and transfer it from the oceans to places in need of water.

This is a moment to acknowledge that everything we are and have comes from our ecosystems. Our very existence and vitality is a product of nature's energies. We are warmed by the sun and cooled by the breezes coming from lakes, oceans, or mountain peaks. Our food is the product of endless interactions among soil, rain, seedlings, and trillions of micro-critters. Then there are those remarkable processes like photosynthesis and genetics!

SCARCITY

Mullainathan and Shafir define scarcity as not having enough of what we feel we need. They illustrate by explaining how malnutrition alters bodily organs, especially the brain. As one's body weakens, the mind loses its capacity to multitask and only attends to the most glaring biological needs. For example, a thirsty or hungry person respectively notices referents to *water* or *food* above everything else. However, at the time, those experiencing such a deprivation rarely notice this propensity. To restore themselves, underfed people need to gradually consume small and balanced amounts of carbohydrates and proteins.[25]

Mullainathan and Shafir characterize economics as the "use of limited means to achieve unlimited desires"—that is, naturally occurring or artificially manufactured scarcity is in the core of this discipline. Even imagining a shortage might occur leads us to act as if that deprivation already exists, as is clear when we fear for our safety. Even in safe environments, mere thoughts about danger produce the bodily, cognitive, and affective responses associated with threat.[26] Scarcity's biggest impact is upon our thinking. It can increase our attentiveness and competence, or it can shrink what we see and prevent important thoughts from even entering our minds.[27]

Scarcity leads people to make trade-offs or fast decisions that can have a positive or a negative outcome.[28] A scarcity such as a tight timeline can increase output. The authors refer to this as a *focus dividend*. When scarcity lowers output, those workers are described as trapped by *tunnel vision*.[29] A mind gripped by scarcity may lead to tunneling or dividends. The conditions are the same for both, so what leads to good outcomes? *Focus dividends* are likely when the key issues are accurately established. *Tunneling* occurs when a single issue is pulled from a set of equally critical considerations and made the sole focus.[30]

It is easy to slip into a scarcity mindset, which draws our attention from other important concerns. That generates secondary and then tertiary scarcities. The authors call this a *bandwidth tax*. What is taxed? It is a person's capacity.[31] If energy in one part of a person's life is used to compensate for other deficits, things get off-kilter. When financial burdens are fused with time shortages, the bandwidth tax increases because each fear generates another fear.[32]

These authors claim that scarcity reduces bandwidth directly rather than injuring people's cognitions. While a person's behavior may look like a cognitive weakness, these economists claim that the source of the scarcity is the context, not the person displaying the deficiency.[33] If a poor performance is not due to an individual's actions, any attempt to fix the person will fail because it is the setting that needs to be repaired. It is easy to make judgments about a person's skills and not see the complexities that individual must manage. A bandwidth crunch tends to occur when work and personal crises collide. Hence, employees who all perform well are not comparable if they have different economic circumstances. The better workers are those who are overtaxed by scarcity's burdens. They are likely to have hidden adaptive skills, greater resilience, and more empathy for others. Since scarcity normally shrinks bandwidth, someone with little slack who is highly productive is probably an unrecognized superstar.[34]

THE BOOK'S ARCHITECTURE

This book has two major structures. The first is conceptual. I discuss abundance in terms of three *domains* or *dimensions* or *strata*, which is how physicists and geologists respectively describe the universe and the earth. I use these terms interchangeably. Domain one addresses four dynamics found in the core of the abundance phenomenon. These are explicated in chapters one through four. Domain two, which are chapters five and six, focuses on how abundance flows into and through human systems. Chapter seven is an interlude linking domains one and two with the third. Domain three, which are chapters eight to ten, explore the processes that help generate and sustain abundance.

The second structure is the design of the chapters. Each starts with a personal story plucked from my experiences. At the time I saw these events as dominated by scarcity, but upon my adopting an abundance outlook, they took on very different shapes and meanings. All stories are followed by a reflection dedicated to grasping the nature of abundance. This personal ethnographic process revealed insights similar to those found in the ancient wisdom literatures, so in each chapter, I draw upon some of the lessons advanced by *Taoism*, *Buddhism*, and *Hinduism*. However, when referring to the wisdom writings, I am not speaking about the religious practices associated with them. The sages of antiquity were addressing existence. Only later did their ideas become a creed-based discipline.

As an organizational psychologist and educator, my hope is that we can all discover the role of abundance in our lives and develop the capacity to learn from our own experiences. Hence, I am using the principles of existentialism to explore the essentials of existence.

I also think that upon inviting others to address life's complexities, authors should make our biases and predilections visible so that readers can decide for themselves what is of value to them.

DOMAIN ONE

The first domain is foundational. At this level, abundance and scarcity are constantly interacting. I refer to this as the scarcity-abundance duo as we examine four processes that are critical to this pairing. Each is accessed via a query.

The *first* issue is *how we get to know abundance. Can it be seen?* Abundance is located within and beneath the manifest, in the deep structures of reality. Like consciousness, it is both in and around everything. However, only a tiny sliver of it is ever visible. So, abundance cannot be seen! While abundance and scarcity exist in nature, they are also concepts that humans invented to explain nature's actions. As with any relationship, when inspecting the abundance-scarcity duo, we are peering into the gaps, at the empty space between the inter-actors. Early in my life I met Maco, a blind student who had a great capacity to grasp the unseen. Chapter one begins with the story of our relationship. During the times we spent together Maco taught me that using only his hearing, smelling, tasting, and touching skills, he was able to "see" much more than I could. This chapter addresses our ways of sensing, and with the assistance of the ancient Chinese notion of *yin* and *yang*, how we can reform our conception of abundance.

If it cannot be seen, is abundance something that can be trusted? This is the theme of chapter two, which is addressed pragmatically. All living organisms are constantly trusting interactions that cannot be seen, like the link between the air and our lungs. Much of our trusting occurs automatically, in *yin-yang-like* realignment processes. This chapter begins with a story of a youth group that decided to build an organization even though they had few skills. They were very successful and managed to create an extraordinary amount of abundance. These teens chose to trust everything, including the value of setbacks, and learned that active trusting increases abundance.

Trusting sets off a chain reaction, which leads into *the issue of faith*, faith in the human rather than the spiritual sense. When ill, do we have faith in the medical system? Do we have faith that the food we eat is safe to consume? Do we have faith that operating according to the principles of abundance will lead to healthy outcomes? That is the theme of chapter three. Here, the scarcity-abundance dance is important. For often a scarcity barrier is necessary to keep things in check, to avoid objects and energies from ending up in unwanted places, like a flooding river. The core question is *whether we have faith in the scarcity-abundance relationship*. Abundance is more profuse when operating in tandem with scarcity, when they are jointly acting to keep things balanced. This chapter begins with an account of a brief medical crisis I once had and my doctor's prognosis, that in order to heal I needed to accept and embrace the scarcity vortex enveloping me!

Chapter four takes the *trust-faith-abundance* triad into the strata of *belief*. Again, this notion of faith is to be viewed in a secular sense. Do we believe a bus driver will take us to the place we want to go, or do we believe that the plane we are boarding is flight-worthy? There are a large number of beliefs undergirding all our actions, even though we may not be aware of them. For educators to be effective, we need to believe in our students' learning capacities. In this chapter, it is evident that the act of believing enhances abundance and that the amplifying of abundance increases our capacities to believe. However, abundance is aided by scarcity's presence, in the same way as a train is well served by the limiting actions of railway tracks and red-light alerts.

This chapter centers on my first job as a teacher of high school students who had almost zero belief in their ability to learn. The educational system, which no longer believed in them, had asked me, a novice teacher, to warehouse them for a number of hours each week. As a twenty-year-old, I refused to accept that there was no hope for them. Ironically, those kids taught me that education is dependent upon the students' and the teachers' belief that learning is possible. If that belief does not exist, the best thing to do is to help develop students' belief in something. I made that my agenda. Those youths taught me how to believe, a lesson found in *Buddhist* thought.

These four issues, sensing, trusting, having faith, and believing, are basic components found in the foundational domain of the abundance phenomenon.

In these four chapters, I introduce what I am calling the abundance-scarcity rheostat, which functions in a manner similar to the *yin-yang* regulator. As the nature of this balancing mechanism becomes clear, it seems that abundance is more about *just-enoughness* than extravagance.

DOMAIN TWO

Abundance is not a thing, nor does it have any solidity. It is as fluid as the wind. It cannot be touched or stored. In the final analysis, abundance is a humanly constructed concept designed to represent the all-pervasive, invisible coursing of energies that sustains existence. This fluidity is the second domain of abundance. While this flowing aspect of abundance can take a number of forms, I have chosen to discuss just two, which I label *streams of generosity* and *rivulets of gratitude*. They are addressed in chapters five and six respectively.

These two themes resonate because most people can recall occasions when they were profoundly touched by someone's unexpected generosity, which in turn activated their gratitude. I chose these forms of fluidity because they can be flowing each way at the same time. For them to be generosity or gratitude, these energies have to be fully received. Without a responsive recipient, they are floating currents in search of a place to be deposited. This particular domain of abundance opens a new vista. It can be summarized by a simple adage: *if there is not enough generosity or gratitude in your life, open your heart.* Then both gratitude and generosity will start flowing in and out of inner crevices we did not know existed. The flowing facets of abundance discussed here are also present in the first and third domains. Chapters five and six delve into several insights found in ancient writings, especially *Hinduism, Buddhism, Judaism,* and *Taoism.*

INTERLUDE

By this point, we will have encountered several times what philosophers have dubbed the *big question*:[35] what is consciousness? And for our purposes here, there are two associated queries: to what extent are we conscious of consciousness, and how can we become conscious of abundance? This interlude plumbs some of the features of consciousness that are knowable, while acknowledging the magnitude of what cannot be accessed by creatures living in this universe defined by fission, fusion, electromagnetism, and gravity.

Since nature is the greatest exemplar of abundance, we pause to explore what we presume to know about the cosmos-consciousness twinship and examine abundance through the parallelisms between scientific findings of the cosmos and the historic studies of consciousness. While this does not answer the *big question*, it sheds some light on our understanding of abundance. The desire for more abundance calls for a change in consciousness, but how can those of us who know so little about consciousness imagine altering that consciousness? This has to be a lost cause. Yet we carry on, assuming that consciousness actually reveals itself to those willing to consider the messages being conveyed.

Chapter seven starts with a story about Australia's indigenous people, who have a comprehension of nature that is foreign to modernity. The affiliated incongruities provide a pathway into what scientific research reveals about the cosmos, lessons I compare with the findings of studies about consciousness undertaken in the Asian subcontinent and recorded more than two millennia ago. The alignment between the scientific findings on abundance and those created by students of consciousness is breathtaking.

DOMAIN THREE

This third domain has a different character from the first two. By this point, we have found that abundance is all about balance, governed by a network of rheostats that maintain equilibrium. While we still have scant sense of how these regulators work, we can recognize their presence and value. There are many human complexities destined to become grim scarcities if left unchecked. However, at some point, they can be switched and become a source of abundance. This change can happen organically or be activated by external forces. There are many such issues, but for this book, I have chosen just three: belongingness, conflict, and anxiety. I selected these because they are seminal for most of us at various stages of our lives. In my personal past, I could never have imagined that anyone's struggles with conflicts, anxiety, or how to belong in unpleasant settings could be sources of abundance. Discovering how they contribute to abundance requires us to develop a fresh take on these dynamics.

Chapter eight explores the struggle to belong, a universal source of suffering, which results from the angst that creates conflict and the conflicts that create anxiety. This exploration starts with a painful story of a young military man about to be court-martialed. He was accused of being absent without leave because his spiritual practices were out of alignment with standard military protocol. He could have easily been jailed or given a dishonorable discharge. This was stopped from becoming a brutal scapegoating by a reframing of the problem. All parties agreed to address this as an issue of belonging. Although no one was a *Buddhist*, a much-needed change was implemented using *Buddhist* principles that were developed in antiquity.

Chapter nine addresses conflicts that have the potential to be the source of inventiveness or devastation. The opening story is of the battles between two academic adversaries. I, a novice, was one of these combatants. The other was the most senior person in my world at that time. We were each other's nemesis, until a crisis forced us to become combative collaborators and creative companions. Our conflicts never disappeared, but they became like the sparks that produce electricity. At the time, I did not understand how such intense conflict could be so valuable to us individually, jointly, and for those with whom we worked. After analyzing the contours of discord embedded in this account, I turn to a profound treatise on conflict, the *Bhagavad Gita*, an epic poem at the heart of *Hinduism*, penned soon after writing was invented. In the *Gita*, the processes of turning scarcity-producing conflicts into abundance is explicated.

Rarely is anxiety viewed as a source of abundance. It is mostly seen as a malady to be avoided if possible or treated if necessary. There is a vast body of professional literature on anxiety. Writers like Rollo May and Paul Tillich,[36] approaching it from an existential perspective, argued that anxiety is not just a pathological condition but also a normal and universal part of existence. For the average person, anxiety becomes justifiably acute when we are lacking something, like being out of water on a mountain climb or waiting for medical tests indicating if a tumor is cancerous. There is another kind of anxiety that is always with us. When we accept its validity and value, this form of anxiety functions as an ever-present companion that amplifies abundance.

Chapter ten explores anxiety. The opening story addresses my first experience of teaching MBA students. Initially, it was a disaster. Then we uncovered an out-of-sight coagulation of anxiety that was paralyzing us all. The natural impulse of everyone, me included, was to get rid of the anxiety. That did not work! Everything improved when we collectively accepted the anxiety inherent in the learning process. This chapter ends with an account of the *legendary story of Abraham*, who came to be known as the founder of the three main monotheistic faith traditions. Although rarely discussed, this account of Abraham's life is filled with insights about anxiety and its role in creating abundance.

CHAPTER 1

SEEING WITHOUT EYES

Can we *see* abundance and scarcity? That is the theme of this chapter. On the surface, this might appear to be a trivial query. But it is more complicated than meets the eye.

Scarcity is evident when stores sit empty in advance of a hurricane or if water is rationed during a drought. Likewise, nature's abundance is on full display at harvest time or upon being drenched by a monsoonal downpour. However, even amidst great lack, images of the plentiful are present. They are tucked inside our expectations that once the tempest's carnage is cleaned up fresh produce stands will be restocked and that water restrictions will end when the wet season arrives. Similarly, summer's bountifulness is a sharp contrast with winter's lifelessness. Strangely, scarcity and abundance seem meaningful only when set side by side. Certainly, these concepts are so linked in our minds it is hard to define one without evoking the other. When abundance is not visible, it is often hidden under scarcity's shroud. And the converse!

Then there are marvels we never see directly, like photosynthesis or radio waves. We notice their effects when eating fresh fruits or searching for a channel playing our favorite music. Also, there are things like the invisible ozone layer, which shields earth from the sun's harmful ultraviolet radiation but enters our awareness only when increasing numbers of skin-cancer patients suggest a new ozone hole has formed. While we have indicators about photosynthesis, radio waves, and the ozone, we do not have senses that can see them directly.

Since sight determines much of what we understand, it is beneficial to know its strengths and weaknesses. While our visual capabilities are impressive, they have major limitations. Of course, we do have technological instruments that provide information about things we cannot see. And we share this planet with creatures that have very different sensory capacities. So, it is wise to also absorb the ways they experience our shared surrounds. While there are advantages to using multiple sensory systems and devices, they also produce perspectives that often appear contradictory. That means we need good cognitive skills to sort out the primal and the peripheral.

My interest in the abundance-scarcity symbiosis began when I met Maco, a blind student. So, I will begin our foray into this topic by describing our first encounter. Once the intellectual dust stirred up by his story has settled, I will begin to explore a theme being threaded throughout this book. It is how the seen, the unseen, and the things yet to come into existence shape our understanding of scarcity and abundance. This chapter will end with some insights on this topic conveyed by *Taoism*, which was developed long ago by brilliant Chinese scholars.

SENSING ABUNDANCE

Leaning his cane on the doorjamb of my Melbourne University office, Maco walked toward me, hand outstretched and his eye sockets pointing to the ceiling. After exchanging pleasantries, Maco, one of a 100 students in a course I was teaching, asked if he could skip all my lectures. Many students miss an occasional class, but never had anyone announced in advance his intent to always be absent! He sought my approval to have my lectures recorded, claiming this would help him greatly, saying, "I can get through an hour of you in 15 minutes!" This quip piqued my curiosity. Responding to my surprise, Maco said he speed listened, something still unknown to me.

Wanting to *see* if his claim was valid, I asked him to lend me his recorder, leave, and return in 30 minutes. Pulling an obscure book from my shelf, I read into his machine. Upon his return, Maco pressed his magic button. My voice sounded like a hyperactive cartoon character. While to me all my words sounded garbled, his comprehension of this unfamiliar passage was nearly perfect. He had 90 percent verbal accuracy. I could follow along as Maco recited what I had dictated. Occasionally he skipped a few phrases or reversed the first and last sentences of a paragraph, but overall, his recall was astonishing. I thought I had *seen* everything as an educator. Shaking my head, I mumbled, "Maco, let's change roles. You teacher, me student! How did you do that?"

Maco's belly laugh filled the room. "You people with eyes have a problem! You can't see! Granted, eyes help. And when I was young, I wished I had them. But they also limit your vision. Eyes notice what they can take in but ignore what they can't process."

Cold sweat gathered in the small of my back. Never had I contemplated how our vision registered a fragment of the data and treated it as the totality. Enamored by what eyes enable, I had completely ignored what they overlooked or obscured.

Maco asked me to do something. I scratched my left ear and rotated my right foot.

"You just rubbed your ear and wiggled your foot," he said.

Stymied by the incongruity of a blind man making such astute observations, I asked Maco, "How did you figure that out? How can you see without eyes?"

"We have many senses," Maco began. "Each can inform us of what the eye misses. There are lots of other cues, sounds, odors, air movements, and temperature differentials, which most people don't register. If you lost your sight, you too would develop new ways to see."

Maco rarely attended class, but he regularly came by my office. We discussed many things, but our chats invariably converged on two themes. First was his conviction that the world is filled with shapes, lines, curves, and angles we do not access because we lack the senses and the cognitive acumen to register them. Second was his contention that his sensorium was superior to mine.

A favorite statement of R. D. Laing, the renowned Scottish psychiatrist, was effectively Maco's mantra: *"What* one *sees* depends on *how* one sees!"[1] Our sensing mechanisms involve many processes. For starters, what we see is shaped by the lenses we look through, the vantage point from which we inspect the world and the predefined contours of the mind into which we map our perceptions.[2] If we change goggles, the parapet from which we peer, or our cognitive apparatus, the data absorbed alters. A similar statement could be made about hearing, touching, smelling, and tasting, senses Maco skillfully used. But not me, which he thought was problematic! He relentlessly asserted that our sensory equipment and our brains have to be carefully honed and properly aligned. He also insisted that for me to access and comprehend the full range of olfactory, tactile, tasting, and auditory sensations, I would need to develop a more advanced set of mental grids!

4

Maco and I made a brief visit to the studies on perception of that era. Here are a few of the basics from decades ago, which grabbed our attention during the months of our relatedness.

Every creature's sensory equipment shapes its experiences. A person may be attracted by a flower's colorfulness. Bees may be drawn to its pollen. A bat may treat it as an echo of ultrasound.

How a locale is to be used often defines how it is sensed. For fish, a lake is a habitat. For deer, it is a source of drinking water. For canoeists, it is a place to paddle.

What the world is like depends on the brain's early imprinting. Animal trainers know that tethering a baby elephant to a sapling with a thin twine makes it feel secure. When fully grown, if that elephant is chained to a large tree, it can easily uproot the trunk. But if it is attached to a sapling by string, it will not even try to escape. In maturity, it will stay within the cognitive parameters established during infancy.[3] Similarly, if kittens spend their early weeks in a box with only horizontal black-and-white stripes and no vertical lines, upon maturation they will bump into upright objects like poles. Those raised in cages with solely black-and-white vertical markings manage furniture legs fine but not horizontal surfaces like ledges and countertops.[4]

We trim the world to fit our ways of knowing. If we examine a landscape with one eye, we see it in two-dimensional terms. A second eye makes depth perception possible. What might we see if we had a third, a fourth, or a fifth eye? And what happens when making a two-eyed inspection of reality that needs eight eyes to see properly? Will we misconstrue everything? Or collapse all multidimensional images into three and fail to recognize the others?[5]

Maco's tutelage was enchanting. Being sightless had not sentenced him to a life of sensory deprivation. He urged me to expand my horizons, to recalibrate my sensorium. His view was I manufactured my own scarcity mindset by not making full use of all the sensory tools nature had given me. It was not science, philosophy, or psychology that led me to see that I had loads of unused sensing, thinking, feeling, and intuiting talents. It was a blind student. His message? Not only do we live upon a goldmine called Mother Earth. We are our own unique, unseen goldmine!

A HUMBLING REALIZATION

Every species has a unique sensorium. However, compared with other creatures occupying these same environs, our senses are relatively underdeveloped.

Human vision operates in a 400-to-700-nanometer range of the electromagnetic spectrum. That is a small slice of a continuum extending from the gamma ray pole that is trillions of times shorter than ours through to the radio wave pole, which is trillions of times longer. Each creature with visual capacities has its own segment, either above or below ours. A good example is the butterfly that locates nectar in flowers using ultraviolet light and hence can notice many colors we never see.[6]

We hear sounds in the 20-to-22,000-hertz (cycles of air compression per second) range. There are creatures that hear well below us, like elephants bellowing messages to herd members at a very deep level.[7] In the forest, we may hear an occasional note of a bird's song, of a frog's tuba solo, of a cicada concerto. But we miss the notes in their symphonic and operatic performances that are at higher and lower levels. Some insects, like male treehoppers, vibrate their abdomens and use sensors on their legs to chat with mates, to attract females, or to scare off predators.[8] Crickets can create chirps by speedily rubbing together their wings that are tailor-made for their own species. For example, the 140 groups of North American crickets have their own sonic niches, a uniquely designated frequency like a radio station.[9] I am in awe of the music composed by geniuses, the instruments created by craftspeople, the skills honed by musicians who are constantly rehearsing. But what they play in grand halls is no match for the impromptu recitals performed in nature's music chambers every day by oodles of creatures without a musical score or a conductor.

We humans live within the earth's magnet fields, have scientific knowledge of electromagnetism, can read a compass indicating true north, and can effortlessly switch on an electric light. But we are not aware of sensing these energy systems directly. However, many birds use electromagnetic currents as their GPS, as their guide during annual long-distance migrations.[10]

Our olfactory senses are also very limited. However, all around us are organisms like ants and bacteria that use smell and taste to locate nutrients or to spot adversaries.[11] Ninety-nine percent of all species encounter the environment and communicate via odors conveyed through chemicals (pheromones, allomones, kairomones). Some scents carry intraspecies messages. Others repel antagonists.[12] These compounds are usually aimed at specific compatriots. For example, the scent of sex-seeking female moths can reach males from a distance of a kilometer. On a human scale, that is like Romeo and Juliet sending come-hither pleas from 50 miles away.[13] Ants guarding their nest can quickly activate their warriors by releasing specific odors.[14] Insects seem to be among the operators of nature's Internet that have explicit species-centered IP addresses, passwords, and a social-media-like capability accessible to those bonded by kinship. It is remarkable how abundant the collective sensing systems of all creatures are, despite the limitations of each individual species' sensorium.

This is the irony of sensory skills. Humans' sensing systems are inferior to most species', but we have greater cognitive skills. Other creatures have more sensory capability but less mental capacity. Nevertheless, humans are sustained by many of these creatures, who source our food, convert it into nutrients, clean out our stomachs after a meal, and degrade what is sent to a bio-dump.

In addition, just imagine how much abundance there might be out there in some unknown reality that no creature has even been able to sense!

SENSORY CONTRADICTIONS

When information is gathered via the multiple senses of many creatures, the disparate findings need to be integrated in order for meaning to be created out of them. This synthesizing is difficult if the data is discordant, which is certain to be the case if truly dissimilar sources have been accessed using multiple methods to gather information. In the scientific realm, this is known as *reliability* and *validity*. If there are large incompatibilities in the data, then judgments need to be made about which bits of evidence are more correct, more actionable, and more useful. That leads into territory known by a variety of names, digitalizing, duality, polarization, and either/or thinking. This arena is fraught with many complications. One of the trickiest is well illustrated by the apocryphal story of the master and the apprentice who are sitting on the riverbank.

Breaking a long meditative silence, the master asks the apprentice, "Is this the same river or a different river from the one that was flowing by here yesterday?"

Realizing that water had gushed through these gorges for eons, the novice spontaneously replies, "It is the same river!"

"Are you sure?"

Following a respectful pause, this puzzled pupil says, "Since these molecules have never passed by here before, it must be a different river."

"Are you sure?" the master asks again.

They both return to their contemplative quietude. Hours later, the apprentice exclaims, "Ah, I *see*! It is *both* the same river *and* a different river. Water has always flowed by here but never this particular set of molecules. Its sameness makes it unique. Its uniqueness makes it the same. Because it is ever changing, it is the same. Because it is always the same, it is different!"

For our purposes, there are two lessons to be taken from this tale.

First, an either/or lens focuses vision, pulling sight into narrow tunnels. It increases a sense of scarcity. Both/and seeing, which by definition includes either/or vision, has a wider-angle lens. It can capture the focused-upon *and* the peripherals. It is an abundance amplifier.

Second, is our propensity to look through an either/or lens, a both/and lens, or both? Images alter when we switch from one to the other. Later we will explore the cognitive aspects of either/or and both/and reasoning. For now, the issue is whether we are aware of using either or both of these spectacles. And in particular, if the pictures generated by these different lenses clash, do we categorize them as two contradictory opposites, like agree and disagree or right and wrong? Or do we treat each as being embedded in its opposite?

9

Several things change when looking with a both/and versus an either/or perspective: (1) the picture alters; (2) the focus becomes primarily the relationships between the things that seem contradictory; (3) observers are forced to look at and into the empty spaces between interacting entities as well as the behaviors of the inter-actors; (4) the links between observations and the ways we traditionally represent those observations are reshaped; and (5) the patterns created by the interactions among the creatures, objects or concepts become the most important things to inspect.

SEEING PATTERNS

How do we see the patterns undergirding relationships? Looking at a rock or smelling a rose is simple compared with sensing patterns. For example, it is not possible to actually see the interactions between the sun, the soil, the rains, and a paddock's crop yield. But over time, a farmer makes a map of the relations among such variables and can identify when they are in or out of alignment. Or a psychologist helping a couple rebuild a broken relationship will recognize the significance of *what the duo is **not** saying, what is **not** occurring* in their interactions. The absences often are more relevant than the words spoken or the actions taken. While other observers may not notice these patterns, competent professionals operating off robust theories about humans' or nature's functioning can discern them. This is a specialist art, seeing the relationships between what is observably happening and what could be occurring but is not.

A perfect exemplar of using the either/or and the both/and lenses and of seeing patterns is the well-known concept of *yin* and *yang*, found in the Chinese literatures written 2,500 years ago. They use a single image to represent these two processes. Later we will discuss the insights the *yin-yang* dynamic contributes to the abundance-scarcity dance.

Patients seeking help from practitioners of traditional Chinese medicine learn early on about *yin* and *yang*. The mere taking of the 12 pulses is a tactile indicator of the invisible *yin-yang* patterns occurring in the body's deep structures.

The *yin-yang* symbol refers to natural dualities, complementary forces like light and dark, life and death. *Yin* represents the earthy, darkness, negative, passivity, absorption, the north or shady side of a hill, the south of a river, the feminine. *Yang* signifies the heavenly, light, positive, activity, penetration, the south or sunny side of a hill, the north of a river, the masculine.[15] As *yin* is in ascendency, *yang* is receding, and vice versa. For ancient Chinese philosophers, the *yin-yang* pattern mirrors nature as a whole.[16]

Yin-yang, depicted above, is a circle consisting of two teardrop-shaped halves, one white, the other black. Nested within each is a miniature of the other, which implies that each part holds its opposite inside it, that neither exists without the other. The external circle symbolizes the undifferentiated *unity of all things*. The internal curves indicate the rising and falling waves of *yin* and *yang* adjusting to each other. Night becomes day; day becomes night. Birth becomes death; death becomes birth. Friends become enemies; enemies become friends. All things continuously surface and subside. The emergence of any *thing* is *yin* and its resolution into *non-thing* is *yang*.[17] From *nothing* comes all *things*. In Chinese thought, every *thing* and every *non-thing* is a cyclical playing out of the *yin-yang* dynamic,[18] which is an indivisible whole. Accordingly, the attaching of labels like good and bad to *yin* or *yang* is meaningless.[19]

Yin and *yang* seem like opposites, such as polarities anchoring a dichotomous continuum or seasonal endings and beginnings. However, they are relational and relative. Water is *yin* compared to steam but is *yang* with respect to ice. *Yin* and *yang* are always rebalancing. For instance, a stone dropped in a calm waterhole produces elevated ripples and lowered troughs that radiate outward until they dissipate, leaving a glassy surface. While neither *yin* nor *yang* exist separate from the other, nothing is completely *yin* or *yang*. As extreme *yin* is approached, *yang* starts to grow. Relative *yin-yang* levels are forever realigning. Too much of one dislocates the other. However, altering from one to the other is ordered and occurs at the appropriate time. Winter yields to spring, never the reverse, but only after winter has run its course.[20]

Both Western and Chinese logics affirm that the sense making happening on the surface indicates what is occurring within the manifest. This has been given a variety of names. Chomsky's term is *deep structure*.[21] Maruyama names it *mutually causal processes*.[22] Bohm considers it to be the *implicate order*.[23] Prigogine labels it *order through fluctuation*.[24] The Chinese call it *yin-yang*. All these scholars ask that we attend to the structural dynamics found *within* the manifest forms, even though the data is primarily accessible on the surface.

TIPPING POINTS AND *YIN-YANG* REGULATORS

I think we currently have only a hazy grasp of the *yin-yang-like* regulators that moderate the abundance-scarcity relationship. However, depending on the issue, this switching dynamic can be anything from a delicately poised, hair-trigger tipping point to a large form of oscillation. Three ecological examples provide approximate images of this equilibrating-adjusting process.

One is the typical predator-prey relationship, such as a territory inhabited by rabbits that are the prey for lynxes. When rabbits are plentiful, the lynx population increases but drops with the overconsumption of rabbits. As the number of rabbits shrinks, some lynxes begin to starve, which leads to a decline in their population, enabling the rabbit population to grow again. This concept, called *order through fluctuation*, is central to co-evolutionary thinking. The oscillation, while being deeply troubling for an individual rabbit, helps to create order at the macro level.[25] If an heroic rabbit wants to preserve the long-term survivability of its species, it has to decide whether to escape or to give itself up to be eaten. To make a smart choice, it would need to know what phase the rabbit-lynx oscillation is in, which vector is increasing or declining, which requires a meta-perspective. It is tough for a creature with only a worm's-eye view to get a bird's-eye perspective. Given its limited awareness, a rabbit will do what makes most sense. It will run. Fifty percent of these escapes contribute to the survivability of the rabbit species, but half the time, that act detracts from it. A lynx is in the same situation. Sometimes a lynx will aid the species by going on a starvation diet, whereas on other occasions, behaving glutinously is best.[26]

13

When the rabbits-lynxes plight is applied to the human domain, we find the same issue, such as the supply-demand nexus, so critical for economic functioning. As all businesspeople know, a well-honed rheostat that harmonizes supply and demand can make or break an enterprise. In the short-term, it often seems important to restore equilibrium as quickly and smoothly as possible. Excessive fluctuation is usually seen as disturbing equilibrium and hence should be minimized. However, order can be destroyed if a system hovers close to equilibrium, whereas more extreme fluctuations around that fulcrum may be what are needed to sustain system vitality.[27]

Ecological studies show a similar pattern between animals and vegetation. With the rise or fall of food resources, some animals, like red squirrels, adjust their procreative actions. Eighteen months before spruce-tree cones mature and drop, these squirrels can estimate the availability of food by noting changes in the taste between the reproductive and vegetative buds. This informs them when the food supply will be plentiful or limited, which leads them to adjust the number of offspring to have.[28]

Across the ages, there has been a stark difference in how humans have conceptualized abundance and scarcity. Early Chinese scholars did not think of abundance as having plenty of everything and scarcity as lacking the things we need. The *Taoists* conceived of abundance as the harmonious movement of *yin* and *yang* in a mutually adjusting relatedness, with *all that is* and *all that is not* being in the core of everything. For them, scarcity was an expression of either *yin* or *yang* gaining so much dominance that the other got diminished, throwing everything *off-kilter*. For such thinkers, scarcity is too much *yin*, or inadequate *yang*, or a blockage of the balancing process between them. That is a radical conceptualization to be explored later.

SUMMARY

We end this chapter with a threefold challenge: (1) how to see or measure energy flows among a system's elements; (2) which energies contribute to abundance and which logjams produce scarcity; and (3) how boundaries enabling or limiting flow contribute to the scarcity-abundance dynamic. This chapter addressed the following themes:

- Our sensorium can access only a small fragment of reality.
- The creatures around us sense things we never recognize.
- We can sense with both either/or and both/and modalities.
- Data produced by multiple senses often seem incongruent.
- Information that is conflicting is cognitively demanding.
- Abundance is about both what-is and what-might-be.
- Our senses are not equipped to tap into latent possibility.
- It is more difficult to see what is potentially emerging than what already exists.
- Abundance is found in the empty spaces between interacting entities.
- The abundance-scarcity dynamic is based on flow, balance, and realignment.

The above presumes we can trust what our senses detect. That is our next topic.

CHAPTER 2

TRUSTING ABUNDANCE

This chapter elaborates on the idea that abundance and scarcity are *features of both our sensorium and of the universe being sensed.*[1] Maybe super entities equipped with mega sensory systems could detect all the abundance in the world, so long as it had a gigantic thinking capacity to process what it accessed. Conversely, a group of exceptionally intelligent beings with few sensing abilities would know little about abundance because it would not have sufficient data. Although human senses have severe limitations we do have technical devices like telescopes that help us to detect the unseen. So, in the above assertion, the word *sensorium* should be read as the aggregate of all sensing systems developed by nature, humans, and organisms.

In this chapter, we touch on a two-pronged question. Can we *trust our senses* to give us valid data about the world? If so, is *the abundance and scarcity seen in nature actually real*? Placing the following two thoughts side by side conveys the gist of this query: "In my friend's mountain village, where the forests are evergreen and the skies are always clear, people assume there is enough oxygen for all creatures to breathe easy forever. In our city, where the smog is always intense, it seems that soon catching one's breath will be a competitive process for all of us." In one setting, trusting the air may seem fine, but in another, that would be inconceivable.

We also explore a proposition, that the *process of trusting generates more trust*. This implies that trusting is an expansive dynamic and distrusting is a restrictive force. The act of not trusting narrows both our senses and what we scrutinize, thereby reducing what we absorb. Pared-down information diminishes cognition, which amplifies anxiety. The resultant distress fuels distrust. However, when we act as if trusting and being trustworthy is a virtue, the amount, quality, and depth of the trusting process grows more abundant.

Only by trusting our sensing systems can we notice things like the abundant and the scarce qualities of what we encounter. Distrusting our senses makes that all but impossible. So, should we trust our senses wholeheartedly, cautiously, skeptically, or not at all? If we are always distrustful, we internalize very little. Swinging to the other pole, our sensorium can detect much more than our synthesizing capacities can process, making it tough to prioritize what is best to trust. That leads to a secondary form of scarcity. An alternate option is to doubt everything that our senses access and trust the evidence that proves our predilections wrong.

To illustrate the *trusting abundance phenomenon*, I recount the experiences of a lackluster youth club that got challenged to unlock its creative energies. These teens chose to do something beyond their competency level. They banged into many scarcity barriers that they dealt with head-on. In the face of impossibility, they acted boldly. When consumed by doubt, they saw trust as their best option and ended up unleashing an unimaginable amount of abundance. Adopting two of the prompts from the last chapter, we will *look at* the plethora of relationships these teens created and trace the abundant energy cascading through their community.

Again, this exploration will end with a few *Taoist* insights.

THE INNCIDER

In our early twenties, two buddies and I took on the leadership of a youth group in a sleepy hollow on Melbourne's outskirts. Our goal was to focus their energies, foster healthy friendships, and provide a sanctuary for their dreams. These teens were studious, played sports, and practiced their musical instruments.

Inevitably the day came when their energies hit a wall. We asked them to list what would stir their get-up-and-go? Top of the list was Disneyland! On the bottom was a *coffeehouse*. This was the sole viable option, so we decided to build one. Within weeks, we had registered as a nonprofit, recruited some parents to be on the board, and established several work groups. Those creating a business plan decided to serve waffles, coffee, etc., with hot nonalcoholic cider as the featured item. That led us to call the place the *INNcider*. We rented the floor above a local store with a capacity for 100 and built a kitchen and a fire escape.

The price tag was huge! Our teens decided to door-knock the neighborhood, selling what they called $100 INNcider shares. There were two provisos: to spread the economic risks, a family could purchase only one share; we would buy back the shares out of our profits. Start-up costs required 25 percent of the local families to invest. These kids' spirits were so contagious, people were soon seeking us out to buy our shares. In no time we had the needed funds.

The facility functioned as a coffeehouse on weekends and a student study center on the other evenings. All labor was donated, with jobs being regularly rotated. We built a musicians' stage and many bands performed here in public for the first time. The INNcider was so successful we had repurchased all the shares within a year and henceforth were debt-free.

However, something unpredictable happened that changed the landscape and character of our cozy enclave. The city's biker gangs, tailed by the police, discovered us. Three worlds began colliding: gangs, police, and a bunch of naïve youths. The INNcider was perpetually full, with 100 patrons outside angling to get in. Due to a law requiring bars to close at 10:00 pm, many of those seeking entry were in desperate need of coffee!

What our youths did astounded us adults. Ignoring the potential problems, they welcomed the bikers! Hence, members of rival gangs were often inside the coffeehouse at the same time. Frequently, two warring, leather-clad groups were backed up against the walls, knives drawn, readying for a fight, with one of us walking between them trying to squelch the overheated passions. Managing these moments was tough, but our teens rose to the occasion. They dealt with it by inventing what they called their *policing policy* and their *flower warfare* strategy.

This was what we negotiated with the legal system. The mayhem created by these gangs attracted considerable police attention, which exacerbated the tumult. So we asked the officers to intervene only if we called them. They agreed but insisted on having paddy wagons circling nearby. We installed a switch on the INNcider music system that simulated approaching sirens. Once activated, people instantly stopped what they were doing. We managed to convince both the warring bikers and the police that we would call law enforcement only if necessary. That proved to be less often and much later in the process than was customary for the constabulary.

The flower strategy emerged organically. The first night that two groups reached for their switchblades, Rowena, a spunky 16-year-old grabbed a bunch of roses she had bought for her grandmother. She gave one to each guy holding a knife. Rowena, a petite gal, was ideal for this task. Anyone could have done her in with a single blow, but she was the kind of lass every red-blooded male hoped would like him. So, as she handed out roses, all action froze. The scene was comic, guys holding a weapon in one hand and a rose in the other, dazzled by Rowena's refusal to be intimidated, not knowing what to do with rose or blade. That gave us a few moments to kick into deal-making mode. Henceforth, we always had flowers on every table!

Our teens learned to manage these kafuffles. Most places wanted these urban warriors banished so our acceptance caught them off guard. In partnership with the gangs' leadership, we created ground rules about fighting that would keep everyone safe and not wreck anything. This was the pact: it is OK, even honorable, for gangs to fight; to be legitimate, battles had to be arranged within the INNcider; all fights would take place in the parking lot across the street; the fights had to be bare-chested, using only fists; the contest would be between two individual warriors chosen by their own gang; the fight was over on sight of first blood; the defeated gang would cook and wait tables for the next hour, plus pay for the victors' food and drinks.

These events became ritualized. Once a fight was arranged, the INNcider emptied out and spectators formed a human cordon. As the warriors were being chosen, the crowd would take sides. The gangs' leadership regulated the fight. If opponents fought dirty, others stepped between them. Seldom did these fights become a melee, and only once was anyone hospitalized.

The police appreciated the INNcider. Having all the gangs in one place made the rest of the city safer. Rarely did the police intervene, and on the occasions they were called, we advocated for those in trouble. This increased everyone's investment in our conflict-management methods. Many patrons had come directly from the bars, so we were always handling the inebriated. We would pump as much food and coffee into these guys as possible, trying to sober them up before remounting their bikes. The next year, several gang members were elected to our management group, which led to rivals working side by side in the kitchen as volunteers. The local florist, upon learning how we handled conflicts, donated all the flowers we needed.

Quite often a guy hoping to elude a fight would grab a flower from a vase and hand it to his adversary. This would trigger a retort: "You're doing a Rowena on me!" If she was in the building, Rowena would step forward and curtsy, accompanied by a rousing cheer.

One night all the local storefront windows were smashed. INNcider was hauled before the municipal council to explain this debacle. After laying out the whole picture, we thought the INNcider might be forced to close. At a pivotal point however, as the council was poised to decide our fate, some members of the local chamber of commerce showed up. They vouched for us and offered to pay for replacement windows. Instead of being blamed, our youths were thanked for what they were doing. This impressed INNcider's adversaries, who later became stalwart allies.

Eventually we realized most of these fights were initiation rituals. It is hard for young males to curtail their anger, especially those who could not access culturally acceptable venting mechanisms. In the Melbourne of that era, many males learned to express and channel their emotions via a wild, intensely physical sport called Aussie Rules football. Others funneled it into fights. There were few options between these extremes.

INNcider's partnership with the gangs made us participants in this developmental stage of young men who rarely let others enter their emotional worlds. The INNcider and these gangs tangoed together for two years. The community grew proud of its teens. And urban policing became a little easier.

It was uplifting to see youths refusing to buy into conventional views of conflict or the injurious labels given to the socially shunned. They viewed gang members as "Just like us. None of us have a clue about how to build a life! So, let's just hang out in the same place and learn how to treat each other kindly!" Our INNciders had no wish to make anyone an outsider.

I will reflect on and integrate this story into the topic of this chapter by focusing on two main themes. (1) *Abundance-scarcity* can be *sensed* and *trusted*. (2) The *process of trusting is self-generating*. Trusting creates more trust. Distrusting begets mistrust.

SENSING THE UNSEEN

First, where in the INNcider story can abundance-scarcity be *seen* or *sensed*? Can those senses be trusted to provide valid data? What can be learned about abundance and scarcity from this community's experiences?

"I'll believe *that* when I *see* it!" This is what several business-savvy community members said when our INNcider youths decided they would try to make a go of it by themselves. What does this mean, "we only believe what we can see?" Only occasionally is this about literal seeing. It is mostly code for "I cannot intellectually or emotionally trust" whatever! Business sophisticates are fairly accurate when calculating the resources needed to build an enterprise that will make sufficient money to pay the bills. However, their financial worksheets do not account for the value of people's unused but readily accessible, noneconomic energies. And there are always folk who see the hidden value in things where success is not even treated as relevant. There is quite a distinction between *seeing what is* and *seeing what is possible*, between *trusting* what is *literally seen* and trusting what is *invisible* but *might become manifest*.

Sensing is the way we encounter our external landscapes. But sensing is also the term used to describe how we access inner panoramas. Seeing an external object or event is nothing like seeing what is inside us. Internal seeing, *in-sight*, is about intuiting, guessing, supposing, grasping, inferring, and tapping into intangibles. We may use sensory language, but we are being metaphoric not literal when we speak of *listening* to an inner voice, of *being touched* by an emotional event, of *sniffing* danger.

Insight combines many processes, but it has a heavily cognitive component. Despite that, it is difficult to know whether the person is having the insight or if the insight is having the person! Sometimes insights and intuitions erupt from an inner place that is much deeper than cognition. On other occasions, they appear to flow into us from an outside source. Every now and then they are experienced as simultaneously coming from within and without. Although sensory terms are abstractions when used to describe inner processing, they do refer to real things, thoughts, or feelings that can be studied. Substantiating this form of sensing, however, requires information that is very different from what is gathered during our I-only-believe-what-I-can-see moments.

The portion of inner sensing that is primarily cognitive is commonly called *connecting the dots*. This is both a pattern-recognition activity and a pattern-creation activity. There are many ways to connect dots, and each arrangement produces different shapes, generates different ideas, and sparks different actions. A pattern is an integration of many things, thoughts, data, emotions,

23

intuitions, and presumptions. That raises the issue of whether a specific combination of dots is an attribute of the realities being explored or a feature of the dot-tethering process. It is definitely the latter. Many people speak about connecting the dots as though those dots already exist and are a representation of reality. That is false! The people or mechanisms doing the sense making create both the so-called dots and the patterns emerging from those connected dots.

This poses the question of what is a dot? That is a silly term, but since this colloquialism is familiar, I will use it for this moment. A dot is not a thing but a representation of something. In the coffeehouse setting, the dots could be viewed as the entities, the gangs, the INNcider, the police, the local council, etc. Each conceived of itself as having its own distinct agendas, unique insights, and divergent priorities. They all managed their own internal parts, their microdots, as it were, and each was also an actor in a set of relationships that morphed into a collective dot-combining system. In this context, there was a web of relationships within and among entities that required a large number of *trusting* actions for the INNcider and its partners to coexist.

An entity can connect its own inner microdots in a constrictive way and relate with others in a scrooge-like manner. Or it can work to elevate itself and its partners. All entities influence their own levels of bounteousness or paucity. However, that is only one part of the process.

Entities filled with abundance or scarcity can infect, for better or worse, their primary relationships. The inter-system dot-creating process is tough sledding when all entities, all dots, are locked into a scarcity mindset, for one outfit's rigidities can set off others' unyieldingness. The opposite is the case when all entities operate off an abundance platform. In most situations, there is a mixture of scarcity-abundance modes of interacting. However, when the parties do the dot-making jointly and adapt to each other's realities, the contagion has a better chance of fostering abundance. This is because the energies can flow freely into, through, and among the entities. When energies are blocked and hindered from flowing, it results in a scarcity scenario.

As the INNcider evolved, the three primary outfits did their sense making within the ever-developing gang-INNcider-police web. This was aided by the teens' tolerance for considerable chaos, which allowed many dots to remain unconnected until all parties had adapted to each other's modes of functioning.

The INNcider acquired several insights about what happens when an entity trusts its inner sensing systems. (1) Trusting abundance unleashes abundance. (2) Senses generate robust and dependable data only when tested. (3) Senses atrophy if left unused. (4) Placing trust in our senses surfaces valuable data, even if it is later found to be inaccurate. (5) Not trusting our senses informs us of nothing save our reticence to trust. (6) To develop trust, there really is no option but to risk failure and count on being able to recover from it if our actions prove fruitless.

The teens running the INNcider were willing to exist in a cauldron of constituencies filled with incompatibilities. They also saw no virtue in responding to setbacks by blaming others. When their initiatives were blocked, they sought a way around the impediment. If something did not work, they moved on.

As they accumulated successes and failures, their energy system grew larger and more nuanced. Trust itself is an energy system that catalyzes more energy. And distrust is an energy sinkhole. The INNcider often acted like a newborn foal that instinctively jumps onto its legs, tries to use its yet-to-be-developed muscles, and flops to the ground. These falls inform an infant animal that not falling is a possibility, if it keeps making an effort. Like young foals, our teens kept falling over. They just got up and tried again, using previously unknown intellectual and emotional strengths. If we consider the foal image as a metaphor, these youths had instincts and capacities that were only ever going to develop if they tried to exercise them. Our INNciders were gradually becoming like galloping horses!

TRUSTING: A CONTAGIOUS PROCESS

The second theme is that the very *process of trusting is self-generating*. Trusting increases the amount and the flow of the trusting dynamic. Distrusting produces more mistrust.

It is rare during a start-up for wholesome instincts to develop. The imperative to be successful is usually so important that metrics based on success dominate. The INNciders trusted that things would work out, and when they did not, these young people refused to fret over any failure. They used setbacks as a prompt to develop more trust in themselves and their partners. Their work units relied on one another. Problems among themselves were rare, in part because they all knew how ignorant they were. For them, everything was an adventure of discovery. Despite their naiveté, or maybe because of it, these groups trusted each other enough to work collaboratively. Their form of co-laboring generated both more trust and more collaboration.

Most astonishing was how speedily these unsophisticated youths raised so much capital. The parents of INNcider members happily invested, but they were only a small segment of the community. Obviously, most moms and dads will buy into their teens' dreams, because the things children do touch their maternal and paternal hearts. Projects like this give parents a peek at what their youngsters are becoming. Typically, they hope their child-rearing behaviors will produce vibrant, functional adults, so it is a gift to witness their own trust-filled parental behaviors being expressed in the maturation of their offspring. In addition, when community members sense something spirit-boosting, they want to be a part of it. This was also a low-grade risk. Spending $100 on such a venture was trivial compared to the money they were about to fork out preparing their teenagers for the workforce or for tertiary education.

The invasion of the bikers was both devastating and awe-inspiring. The shocker was the youths' dreams got shattered. The surprise was how much their trust grew. These teens did not discuss the idea of being hospitable to the bikers. They just instinctively accepted all who entered the building. Rowena, the heroine of the first knife clash, was being her normal self: fearless, confrontational, humorous, and embracing. Via one simple encounter, she showed that anyone could moderate conflict, including the bikers.

Trust-creation's crowning moment was when the INNcider and gang leadership jointly legitimized fighting, designed ground rules for combat, and implemented their tension-releasing mechanisms. A close second was the police-INNcider pact. The officers were rightly reluctant to hand over the reins to these kids. But they accepted the peculiarities of the situation and joined this experiment. Professionally, they were obliged to remain mistrustful. But they operationally acted in trusting ways. Everyone accepted the police could reverse their position if necessary, which led them to be less prone to act.

These youths never strove to build trust. It emerged out of their individual and collective actions! Month by month, trust grew until it was an everyday part of their locale's ethos.

The development of the community's trust was most visible when the storefront windows were smashed. Officialdom could have easily blamed the biker gangs. That would have been incorrect. No one chose that path. The actions of the chamber of commerce were dedicated to simply making the INNcider and the community whole again. As scarcity thinking receded and abundance took center stage, mutual trust became these people's social currency. The florist's daily donation of flowers was far better than any standard marketing plan. And the trusting bond forged between bombastic gangs, a horde of ordinary teens, the police, and a once relatively dull community was worth a small fortune.

When potentially conflicting parties jointly do the relationship-dot connecting, they place more trust in the patterns they create. That elevated trust increases the energies among those relationships for the increased vibrancy lubricates their interactions. In general, when an external authority does the dot connecting and forces it upon the interacting parties, the entities' trust in those patterns is harder to build. Diminished trust elevates the stress. Then barriers get erected to protect the stressed-out parties from the mistrust of others. That reduces the energies incubating within and circulating among those relationships. Blocking the energy flow drains the parties and their relationships, making all entities less robust. In contrast, the amplified energy flow created collaboratively and based on trust sustains those parties and their interconnections, making those bonds more resilient.

LESSONS FROM *TAOISM* ABOUT ENERGY

We now build on the previous discussion about *yin-yang* energies that are highly active but invisible until they become manifest. Recall the *Taoist* conception. Abundance-scarcity is about the balance of energies. Abundance is an expression of the harmonizing ways *yin* and *yang* mutually adjust to one another. Scarcity emerges when either *yin* or *yang* are dominant.

The idea of energy being scarce, be it humanity's or nature's, was not originally a conventional thought, as evidenced by the insights found in *Taoism*, a very sophisticated and old system of thinking.[2]

Taoist logic was passed on via two written streams. One is *Chuang-Tzu*, a manuscript, dated 350–320 BCE. The other is a text that surfaced a few decades later, *Tao Te Ching*, reputedly crafted by an anonymous source called *Lau-Tzu*, which means the *Old Master* or *Old Philosopher*.[3] *Tao's* initial meaning was the *path* or the *way* and evolved into a philosophical method and a course of conduct. However, the *Chuang-Tzu* and *Tao Te Ching* treat *Tao* as being not just a thing, a substance, but the totality of all things and all non-things that are in constant flux but also are simultaneously unchanging, absolute and indivisible.[4]

Most of *Tao's* creative energies are invisible, occurring out of sight, bathed in darkness. To convey this, *Lau-Tzu* uses nature as an exemplar and a metaphor. The Master points to the earth and the wildflowers growing in untended fields, which in winter looked empty, brown, or snow-clad. But in summer they are covered with colorful vegetation, showing that the seeming nonexistence during the barren months was gestating a vitality to be expressed later.

As spring bursts, latent fecundity becomes visible, thanks to the sunshine, rain, bees, ants, chipmunks, etc., living out their individual existence and sustaining many other lives in their multiple, manifest forms. When the blossoms have run their course, the seeming death at summer's end announces the next stage of the cycle as the life visible in the sunlight is returned to the invisible underground.[5]

For each bundle of energy that exists as a manifest anything (plant, insect, etc.) the return to its source is serene. Therefore, an encounter with scarcity is like a punctuation mark, a pause between musical notes in a continuous stream of abundance.

Taoism teaches that every existing thing, at the most microscopic and the most macroscopic levels, is actually energy. The incarnation of these dynamisms in the form of matter should not mask the reality that substance is still energy. So, any discussion about there being inadequate energy in the universe, in beings of all kinds including humans, is a logical absurdity. The universe *IS* energy! We are first and foremost energy! This might seem radical to modernity, but it has been the foundation of human thinking for several millennia. The main issue is releasing or accessing the universal energy and what to do with it once it is in our hands.

While *Taoist* language is very different from the rational, scientific, technological, and regulating terminology that dominates today's vocabulary, this ancient thought form is extremely relevant. It encourages us to trust nature and the messages nature sends us. It invites us to treat the energy system of the cosmos, the *Tao*, as the *Universal Mother*. The image offered is of a great empty womb, which carries in embryonic form a universe of potentialities from which all *things* and *all non-things* emerge.[6]

The choice of the maternal seems on-song; because of all the things in nature that are both scarce and abundant, it is in the realm of birthing that these processes visibly converge. Conception for most organisms occurs in a highly bounded space, as does gestation. As this limited space becomes too small, the newborn bursts out of the shell or the uterine container and into existence.

Yet inside the confined space of those protective walls, the wildest cell-multiplication process had been occurring, making good use of the DNA passed down from more ancestors than any of us could ever count. In addition, the statistical probability of any specific life, like you or me, ever coming into existence is miniscule. Here we see nature's genetic extravagance and its stunning cell multiplier processes.

SUMMARY

This chapter addressed 10 themes:

- Abundance and scarcity are features of our sensorium and the universe being sensed.
- The more we trust all our senses the more knowable our world becomes.
- Trusting is an abundance-generating process.
- Sensing what-is and what-could-be are different processes.
- To know the external or the internal, look at the internal-external relationship.
- In-sights are products of our pattern-creating processes.
- Pattern making can swell or shrink abundance or scarcity.
- Abundance and scarcity are both contagious processes.
- Most abundant energies are invisible.
- Everything IS energy, so there is always enough energy in the universe.

Chapter 3

Healing Relationships

The trust-scarcity-abundance triangular bond is also present in healing, a theme I will enter by recounting a personal medical event. **Symptom**: kidney distress. **Diagnosis:** patient in midst of an emotional shake-up. **Treatment:** recommend patient alter his ways of functioning. For me, this was a debilitating setback that proved to be revitalizing. My doctor's advice was to *have faith in nature's way of curtailing my overzealous aspirations.* A strong biological force had stopped me in my tracks, showing me that scarcity buffers fulfill a valuable function. Without constrainers like dams and embankments, too-muchness is like a gushing torrent or an ever-flooding river.

We now examine an abundance-scarcity dynamic that is normally hidden but sometimes becomes manifest and identifiable at the surface level. As already indicated, it helps to think of abundance and scarcity in terms of movement, velocity, and balance. A waterway's currents are fairly easy to detect. This is not the case with the biological energies inside a body, which are noticed mainly when they get blocked. Again, we encounter the need to have faith in the unseen. The issue is twofold. What is involved in accepting data generated by devices tracking cellular activity, and what does it mean to have faith in the cells upon which existence depends?

This chapter addresses the following: Faith is ever present, contributing to our well-being, at both the psychological and the biological levels. When ill, we automatically become dependent on our immune system and the advice of healing professionals. We rarely know whether doctors' counsel will help, but we place our faith in them anyway. It really is our only option. When trapped by the limitations imposed by sickness, we are prompted to rethink and reprioritize many things, especially how much we take abundance for granted until some scarcity strips us of our normal bountifulness. We may crave to be liberated from our psycho-physical restrictions, but such deprivations do spotlight the abundances we typically overlook and fail to value. Scarcity and abundance are perpetually changing us. That is something we have to accept. The act of placing our faith in the abundance-scarcity dynamic however also alters us. Something similar to this is also occurring at the cellular level, although we are rarely aware of this fact.

At times, the thoughts expressed in the following discussion seem to exceed the bounds of credulity. However, these evolving ideas about abundance-scarcity are in accord with several ancient Asian insights, which are today being increasingly embraced by scientists. We end with a few ties between abundance-scarcity and the medical practices spawned by *Taoism*.

A CURATIVE CRISIS

I had not seen my father since my mother's death. For months, I felt torn between my wish to visit him, to care for our young family, and to meet my work obligations. One night after teaching my last class for the week, I headed to Australia, a thirty-hour journey each way. I hoped to spend three days with my dad, who resided in an assisted living facility. While being ambulatory and engaged, his Parkinson's disease and memory losses had left him disoriented. Thinking some outdoor time would help, we drove to a seaside village where his sister lived. Our family often vacationed in this slice of paradise, so our hour-long trip from Brisbane was filled with recollections of yesteryears. Sitting atop a 40-foot craggy cliff, my aunt's home overlooked the Pacific Ocean where the sights and sounds of thunderous waves were a stark reminder of nature's power.

Soon after arriving, I became doubled up with pain. My aunt called for a taxi. As I crawled into the cab, I begged the driver to drop me off at the nearest hospital. With the classic Aussie drawl, she said bluntly, "No point going there, mate! Not for a person as crook as you! They have few staff. It'll be hours before you see a doc!" Approaching the village center, she pointed to a doorway, saying, "That's the local doctor's place. Go in and ask for help."

Although the waiting room was full, a nurse whisked me into a cubicle. Within minutes, Dr. Silver, a woman in her 40s with an Earth Mother persona, was examining me. A quick diagnosis led her to conclude I had a kidney stone and required hospitalization. Painfully, I downloaded my story. "I am flying back to the United States tonight. I'm here with my elderly father. We are visiting his sister, who I guess is a patient of yours. I have a rental car that has to be returned to the airport tonight. My airline ticket is not refundable. We have two-year-old twins, and my wife is pregnant. I have to teach soon after landing in Philadelphia. Please medicate me, so I can catch my flight. I'll get treated later!" I felt breathless from sucking up the pain long enough to spit out those few facts.

The doctor in a kindly tone repeated that I must be hospitalized, assuring me that she would take care of everything. One shot of a palliative and I departed consciousness. As I came to, Dr. Silver said, "I have your wife on the phone. You can talk with her. But first, this is what I've set up. I have reserved a bed for you in a good city hospital. A urological specialist will manage your care. I called your airline. With no extra charge, they will give you a seat on the first flight after you recover. Your aunt has arranged for her niece to return the rental car. Your brother will meet you at the hospital and take your dad to his residence. Soon we will X-ray you to confirm my diagnosis. In three hours, a taxi will pick up your father, come here, and take you both back to Brisbane."

Dr. Silver's care disarmed me. She was treating all parts of my being, including my whole life context, confident that all would be fine if I could let go of the burdens I was carrying. The way she reshaped my circumstances was exactly the help I needed. "Here's your wife," she said, handing me the phone. My chat with Sara was very comforting.

Upon the taxi's arrival, Dr. Silver helped me into the vehicle, and as I joined my dad, she handed me an invoice for about US $100, in today's terms. I was stunned that such compassion could cost so little! My brother met us at the hospital. He took care of our dad. And I was loaded onto a gurney.

After being connected to an intravenous drip, encouraged by three ward-mates, I started downing liters and liters of water. Thirty hours later, my kidney stone and I departed company. I caught the next available flight and was home in fine shape, two days later than expected.

This was a minor health event, but this physician's care touched an unrecognized chord in me. Her medical assistance was invaluable. But she initiated a deeper healing by taking in and treating the whole of my life and its distress-filled context. She treated my life, not just a troubled kidney. And once again I was filled with gratitude for the compassionate arms of both strangers and loved ones who have repetitively caught me, lifted me, and cradled me during troubled times.

REDISCOVERING FAITH

Trust is essential to building sustainable relationships, as shown in the coffeehouse case. It was also prominent during this medical crisis, except that here the nature of the relationships and the dynamics were very different. These struggles were not among interdependent entities but between conflicted parts of the self. The distress was expressed via the actions of a single bodily organ.

While that malfunctioning kidney was a problem, it was a symptom, *not the dis-ease.* The real *dis-order* was a life loaded with too many stressors that had become gridlocked. Recovery depended on these psychic pressures being dealt with in unison. That required having faith in a letting-go process. It was time to change *my way of being*! I had pushed the limits in many domains of my life, and something had to give. The ejection of that stone brought an end to my juggling act. Fortunately, Dr. Silver knew my biosystem would self-correct once I stopped refueling my self-made tornado.

The term *healing* derives from a Greek word, *holos*, which means *whole*. When the whole person is being treated, the scarcity-abundance dichotomy subsides as limits imposed by illness open paths to new forms of wholeness. In this sense, dis-ease is part of a story about an emergent transformation, even if the endpoint is death.[1] In my case, Dr. Silver and my urologist made an accurate diagnosis and managed my pain. However, their major doctoring was getting me to lie down and drink buckets of water! In one sense, that was all they did! However, it was much more!

They helped me surrender, knowing that I would become whole if I was prepared to have faith in nature's healing ways and to accept that my scarcity-filled mini-crisis was both a limiting event and a time of renewal. This pair of thoughts are two threads being woven into the logos of this book: what flows from increasing one's capacities to have faith in nature's ways; and how can the scarcity produced by illness be an abundance incubator?

Having faith in both abundance and scarcity is key. At a surface level, it seems desirable to seek and relish abundance. However, in the realm of healing, bountifulness and boundedness act in tandem, with restraining structures often serving as a healthy container. Scarcity regularly builds boundaries in a manner similar to how skin keeps our innards inside, how caves provide shelter from tempestuous elements, and how cocoons nurture nascent life. Suffering indicates something of import is occurring. It is natural to want a pain-free life. However, pain is as crucial to wellness as an emergency light is to an aircraft's safety. It is foolish to dismiss distress signals. Ignoring danger signs never nullifies a potential hazard.

Restrictive structures are very important when there is a contagious disease, and normally permeable boundaries have to be closed. Quarantining an infected area is the opposite of what is beneficial when there is a positive contagion, as with the INNcider. Endless possibilities and wide-open spaces are great but can also be more paralyzing than the limits imposed by scarcity.

Existence calls upon us to have faith in scarcity and abundance. Separately and together, both are important. Each can elevate or depress the other. Each can keep the other in check. However, it is hard to simultaneously trust both these contradictory conditions! Which should we have faith in and under what circumstances?

This is difficult to determine using standard logic, but when using *Taoist* reasoning, the contradictory feature of opposites fades. As previously discussed, early Chinese scholars did not conceive of scarcity as crippling shortages and abundance as bloated extravagances. They saw both as a manifestation of a flow. In their paradigm, scarcity prevails when either *yin* or *yang* is so dominant the other is relatively weakened, thereby subverting the flow and disrupting whatever is linked to those currents. Framed this way, scarcity exists when the *yin-yang* balance is impeded due to there being too much *yin* and insufficient *yang*, or vice versa. Abundance abounds when *yin* and *yang* harmoniously adjust to each other, enabling the right amounts of both *yin* and *yang* to coexist.[2]

Thinking in terms of flow raises again the theme introduced earlier: how do we see or sense flow? What are the right vantage points for making observations? And where in the stream of ever-altering events can calculations about its volume, directionality, and rapidity be made? This is especially difficult if the observers are actually in the stream. As Einstein's theories of relativity imply, those who are part of the flow could only notice the quantity, quality, and speed of flows if they are compared with what stationary observers would register. However, external witnesses need to be in the stream to know the key moments to make measurements!

Eastern philosophy helps clarify the role of faith in the abundance and scarcity found in healing moments like my mini-medical hiccup. That stone's ejection shattered a pattern needing to be broken. I had been determined to keep my pressure-filled challenges segmented, to address them sequentially. Dealing with them at the same time would have paralyzed me. That is what happened. I banged into a scarcity block, which was my undoing and my liberation. The task was to let go of the attachments reinforcing dysfunctional patterns.

A few *Buddhist* insights throw light on this topic. Eyes are equipped to scan only the surface of already existent objects or happenings. So, it is hard for them to notice the coexistence of all things, the scarcity-abundance balance, the *yin-yang* adjustments, the bonds among objects, or the happenings at the deep levels. Nor can eyes take in that *almost everything substantial is invisible.*[3]

To address this, *Buddhism* suggests there are several forms of seeing, each of which has to be cultivated. One, called the *Dharma* eye, attends to the boundaries that make objects appear separate and unique. Another, the *Taoist* eye, focuses on what binds things. A third, the *Buddha* eye, sees without making distinctions between *what is* and *what is not*, between what seems to have form and the emptiness surrounding it. *Buddhists* treat *being* and *non-being* as two parts of a whole. They also do not give credence to space and time. For them, there is no difference between *here* and *now* or *there* and *then*, viewing everything as happening in the eternal now. They see each being and each object as a place, a position, a point in a universal flow.[4] That flow is not singular, however. It can be mutiple streams regulating one another, contouring possibilities, or engendering cacophonies. These are thoughts from antiquity that are highly aligned with concepts like quantum and relativity.

It is easy to be captivated by the surface appearances and to ignore the inner realm where nothing is visible. For 2,500 years, via its reflective methodologies, *Buddhism* has shown how to grasp both the exterior and interior features of objects and happenings. During meditation, when looking outward, externalities seem to extend into infinitely distant domains. Looking inward, the internalities descend into infinitesimally small realms. Due to technology, this is now scientifically testable. Repetitively switch between looking at the stars though a telescope and at the tiniest of particles through a microscope. Rotate this process rapidly between scanning the macrocosm and the microcosm and it is hard for observers to know if they are looking at the gargantuan or the miniscule. The deep structures of the macro and the micro are basically identical.

Buddhism asserts that at the boundary where inside and outside worlds converge, three forms of awareness surface: every thing and every being is simultaneously part of something that is both tiny and gigantic, all things are interconnected, and an individual's mind is but a small segment of the universe's intelligence.[5] At this mini-maxi vortex, a form of *transcendence* is noticed that can seem mystical. This numinous sense easily arises upon tumbling into the mysterium. However, it is similar to being soul-touched while witnessing a sunset or seeing the seasonal migrations of birds or watching whales swim large distances to suitable spawning spots.[6]

HAVING FAITH IN OUR BIOLOGICAL SYSTEMS

Our existence as biological creatures depends on the connections among our sensing capabilities, a sophisticated trusting dynamic, the healing process, and the abundance-scarcity dance. This unifying network is unseen. Yet every being's wellness rests upon it. This is the punch line. *Our life is made possible because we are constantly dying at the cellular level* (scarcity), ***AND*** *at the same time we are being biologically reborn* (abundance).

Many things occur within our bodies all the time, a small number of which result in illness, but most of them keep us well. We are only alive because our biological system is both always dying and coming to life. This is the startling story, which we know thanks to powerful technological devices. *Each year, almost all of our body's cells reproduce themselves.* We get a new skeleton every few months. We acquire new skin every month. Our stomach cells are replaced every few days.[7] The red blood cells flowing through our bloodstream are renewed every few months. This means millions of fresh cells are formed in our body every minute.[8] In a few moments, many present parts of us will not even exist.

Scientists estimate that the average human consists of at least 30 trillion cells.[9] We also have just as many bacteria passing in and out of our bodies. In a sense, each person is an ecosystem for lots of micro-critters. The amount of cellular dying and being born anew is astonishing, but it is this ongoing process that perpetuates living. Amazingly, our bodies are never in a static state. There is a phenomenal amount of both abundance and scarcity tangoing inside us all the time.

Although we may see ourselves as being in a relatively stable condition, each of us is a veritable river of change. No time between the cradle and the grave are we in a fixed condition. We are always in a state of decay and renewal. Being healthy does not mean we are not sick. It means we are always being healed. Illness and death are core components of the life force and are as much a part of our living as those things that appear to be wholesome.[10]

The strange part of this story is that, without being aware of this, we are constantly having faith in our biological system. We count on it and yelp when it fails us. Both scarcity-inducing and abundance-increasing activities are always occurring within our beings. Although we rarely think of this, we consistently count on the faithfulness of the cells that make up our bodies.

Our cells also rely on the trustworthiness of the cells they interact with and the bio-ecological system within which they are embedded. These cells that enable us to exist do not overly cling to life. They trust their fate and act as if their brief lives are all important. They also act as if whatever they pass on to the next generation of cells will work out just fine, having previously accepted what their ancestor cells faithfully bequeathed to them.

A critic might protest that cells cannot be thought of as acting in a trusting or faithful manner because things without consciousness could never be described as engaging in such psycho-philosophical acts. That is a fair comment! But we humans, who claim to be conscious, place our faith in many things we have zero knowledge of and that are never in our awareness. This is evidenced by how we unequivocally rely upon our immune systems. Most of us have no idea about how this works, but we have faith in its restorative and health-sustaining powers.

One possible approach to health care is to daily celebrate all that is operating well. Even if something is wrong, it may involve only .0001 percent of our biological system. So, it might be wasteful to obsess over our hobbled, sleepy, diseased, and maimed cells because every person is infinitely healthier than sick! When a medical system is based on detecting what is going wrong, if nothing is found to be malfunctioning, the usual assumption is that everything is OK. That is false logic. The absence of bad news is not evidence of good news.

Consider the fact that our bodies produce cancer cells every day. Fortunately, our bodies have built-in self-corrective means to ensure that the cells do not proliferate too quickly. So, being able to track the ongoing viability of our immune system is valuable. Is failing to find something broken the only way to know what is functioning? Surely it would be much more useful to explore directly how well our reparative systems are doing and if they are asleep or lethargic to wake them up or give them a boost. The importance of sustaining an immune system's functionality is now considered all-important in virtually every medical field.[11]

Upon examining human behavior, we notice that although claiming to have consciousness, we constantly place our faith in the trusting and trustworthy actions of the cells that make up our bodies while remaining mostly unaware that we are doing this. Trust seems to be in the core of our biological beings even though we may think trusting is something we actively do. The story in the biological domain is not whether the activities to which I am ascribing the term *trust* are occurring. They are. However, that usually becomes noticeable only when impediments block or hinder the normal trusting dynamics.

This is in evidence with autoimmune disorders when some cells mistakenly set out to destroy healthy tissue, which is usually due to a breakdown of intercellular communication. In general, immune system blood cells provide protection from potentially harmful intruders, like bacteria, toxins, or viruses that carry antigens. It is the immune system's task to create antibodies that can fend off threatening antigens. However, sometimes the agents tasked to keep us well fail to distinguish between antigens and healthy tissue. That mix-up leads the body to mistakenly attack the cells it is designed to defend. The result is a breakdown of established reliabilities, and cells can no longer trust each other to act in accord with the body's requirements.[12]

Using immune diseases as a metaphor, if we step back and investigate our habitual actions, it is obvious that humans often place their faith in flimsy or ridiculous things society wants us to value, like fame and fortune. Such illusions are dangerous. As we debunk such delusions, it is easy to cease having faith in the very process of trusting itself. Hence, we all need reminders that even as we shun fake news, political rhetoric, or whatever, essentials like the breath filling our lungs and loving one another are everlastingly central to the structure of faith.

A *TAOIST* FORM OF RESTORATION

Here are a few *Taoist* thoughts to help us on our way as we bridge to our next topic. Any foray into Chinese medicine brings a seeker of insight face-to-face with *Ch'i*, a core component of this ancient land's cosmology. *Ch'i* is a term symbolizing *vital energy* or *life-breath*, which is tied to *yin* and *yang*'s mutual-adjustment processes. The *Ch'i-yin-yang* trifecta is the *Tao* in action and, as such, is the heart of regeneration.[13]

Existence involves a balancing of opposites, of contradictions, of polarities. At the center of the *Tao*, there is a void, an emptiness filled with rejuvenating energy, provided the polarities are not overly clung to and are released in the right ways at the right time. The hanging on and the letting go of both *yin* and *yang*, along with the moderating influences of *Ch'i,* contribute to creatures' well-being.[14] *Ch'i* acts as the driver of everything and as the preserver of the balance between polarities. Its role in all the body's *yin-yang* activities is to help synchronize dissonances.[15]

With training and practice, individuals can learn to move their *Ch'i* into specified regions of the body, thereby assisting the normal *yin-yang* balancing. This usually requires the aid of a guide, yoga, martial arts, meditation or acupuncture.

Acupuncture is based on *yin-yang* patterns and the flow of *Ch'i*. Practitioners of this craft strive to make realignments, preserve balance, and release blockages, thereby helping the respiratory, digestive, and circulatory functions. They work to support the cycles from which nature's permanence is fashioned.[16]

This tradition, based on centuries of observations, draws upon elements found in nature, namely earth, wood, metal, fire, and water, along with their interrelatedness, which are described as existing in two cycles, called generating and conquering successions. In the first rotation, wood spawns fire, fire generates earth, etc. In the conquering interchange, wood overcomes earth, earth dominates fire, etc.[17]

The relations among these eco-elements, the component parts of every organism, along with these generative and conquering dynamics, are linked to anatomical organs of humans that fulfill either the body's internal *yin* functions (liver, heart, spleen, lung, and kidney) or the external *yang* functions (gall bladder, small intestine, stomach, and large intestine).[18] This helps thinkers to view interruptions to something like the kidney function to be expressing a specific form of *yin-yang* imbalance.

I am grateful for the insights Chinese philosophy and healing professionals offer, but the validity and utility of this paradigm is way beyond my capacity to adequately grasp. My purpose in addressing this tradition is not to praise or critique it but to highlight how faithfully the ancients mapped and passed along their ideas about living in harmony with nature. The message is when humans are aligned with nature it is possible to experience abundance. When we try to dominate or fight against nature, that battle is primarily a war with ourselves, which we are certain to lose. For the feud itself locks us into a scarcity mindset.[19]

Long after my kidney stone crisis, I understood that event in a new way. The *Taoists* treat the kidney function as filtering the blood and eliminating impurities. This cleansing is both a literal/metabolic and a metaphoric/emotional process tied to a person's ability to detach from disquieting thoughts, unmanageable life situations, and actions not aligned with present realities. Kidneys also anchor energies congenitally transmitted from ancestors that become part of a person's constitution, strength and vitality. Included in this cluster of energies are one's beliefs, sentiments, will, awareness, and purposes.

Taoists also ascribe a spiritual function to the kidney. It carries echoes of who we are and where we have come from. In this regard, the kidney function is linked to our origins. Being preoccupied with fears, insecurities, or apathies that dampen motivation or retard thinking tend to be expressed as a kidney deficiency. An impaired kidney function is metaphysically associated with disheartening disappointments or setbacks.[20]

The occasion of my kidney stone ejection turned out to be the last time my father could recognize me. It was also the first time I had been in my homeland after my mother's death and the sale of our ancestral home.[21] Never again could I return to the emotional time or place that had shaped me. I had entered a major life transition, and there was no turning back. It was time to release myself from some of the things tying me to my origins, so I could dedicate my energies to what Sara and I were creating on the other side of the world. I now think of this medically triggered scarcity as emotionally preparing me for the birth of a yet-to-unfold abundance.

SUMMARY

- Healing begins by accepting what is blocking our health.
- To heal means to make the entire system whole.
- The cells in our bodies consistently trust one another.
- Both abundance and scarcity are about movement, velocity, and balance.
- Faith, taking action in the midst of great uncertainty, is based on the trusting process.
- Abundance abounds as *yin* and *yang* harmoniously adjust to

each other.

- Wholeness depends on the balancing of just-enoughness and not-too-muchness.
- Every lived moment is dependent upon faith.
- Every minute millions of our cells die and millions of new ones are born.
- Placing our faith in abundance is an abundantly healing force.

This chapter leaves us with two challenges: how to develop faith in both abundance and scarcity, and what is involved in learning to believe in phenomena we cannot not see, sense, or fully comprehend?

CHAPTER 4

LEARNING TO BELIEVE AND BELIEF IN LEARNING

All learning is based on faith and belief. Good educators have faith in their students who in turn believe in the guidance their teachers offer them. Students usually believe it is best to acquire maximum knowledge while risking as little as possible. That is smart. Yet the most significant lessons invariably result from substantial risk-taking with few guarantees of success.

Garden-variety belief is present in everyday human affairs. This was much in evidence during the 20th century. An avalanche of twisted beliefs gave rise to Nazism. Belief in human ingenuity led to humans walking on the moon. Contradictory beliefs perpetuated by adversarial nations led to the cold war and the nuclear arms race.

When learning about abundance and scarcity, we face several circularities. Unless we believe in the data indicating the presence of abundance and/or scarcity, we are unlikely to act upon it or test its validity. Hence, we will not learn about abundance and scarcity or how they impact us. Belief in learning increases our knowledge. Newly acquired insights also strengthen and reshape our beliefs, thereby injecting more abundance into our beliefs about learning. This reinforces the desire to learn more.

Belief is not just an individual proclivity. It is closely linked to collective dynamics. Communal beliefs are most impactful when many people interactively create them. Individuals working alone do not understand groups. Understanding a group requires belonging to a group. Similarly, groups cannot truly grasp organizations. For an organization to know its own nature requires system-wide reflecting processes. Likewise, learning about abundance and scarcity, which are collective phenomena, is reliant on a collective methodology.

As we delve into this topic, it becomes evident that learning is healing and that healing is a special type of learning. Hence, insights acquired about learning also apply to healing.

In my professional life, I am often involved in discussions with educators laboring in under-resourced schools and with corporate executives wanting their workforce to perform in prescribed ways. These exchanges usually grind to a halt when senior directors in these institutions make a declaration like the following: "Most people can learn task-based skills and soak up lots of information, but they have little success learning how to deal with their emotions, especially when interacting with people of different backgrounds. However, given the pressures we are under, we can't afford the time to figure out how people learn or how to assist them in their personal or emotional development. So, we just drill them on what they must know to perform well!" Fortunately, my first experience as an educator taught me the exact opposite of what these executives seem to believe. I begin this chapter with my story of that discovery.

Aided by insights about the human condition developed by the *Buddha* and honed by his followers over the centuries, I end this chapter with a strong assertion: faith and belief in both the learning and the healing process are essential to understanding abundance and scarcity.

STUDENTS, PLEASE HELP ME TEACH

The never-to-be-erased feature of my coming-of-age was my first full-time job. With just a BA and not a single course on instructional methods, I became a teacher of math and science at an all-male high school. I was out of my depth! But the spark lit in me that year never went out. Three times I unsuccessfully tried to exit the educational profession. It turned out that tilling the fertile soil of learners became my calling.

"Sorry, sir! Couldn't do me homework last night," announced Jones as I began my second geometry class with 10E, a gaggle of 30 boys, only five of whom had previously passed algebra.

I asked, "Why not?" His cheeky grin spoke volumes. Jones groaned. "I couldn't cotton-on to what I was s'posed to do!" That set off the recalcitrant chorus: "Me neither!"

I mumbled, "None of you did it, right!" I knew a gang-tackle in the making! Only a few years earlier, this was how I was behaving!

"I did it," came a meek voice from somewhere. "Boo," snarled the back-row crew.

"OK, OK," I declared, "this is my testing day. I get it!"

"No testing, sir! This is for real! We are the thick-skulled class. Come on, sir. They must have told you! Don't pull our legs. 10A are the geniuses. 10B are the bright ones. 10C are the regulars. 10D are the we-ain't-giving-up-on-them-yet kids. We're 10E, the *no-hopers*! That's why we got you."

I was in that iconic stand-and-deliver situation. At the end of that year, all 10th graders had to take statewide exams in eight subjects. In that Australian state back then, only students who passed at least six of these grueling tests were permitted to continue their schooling.

The history of 10E's maths both depressed and stimulated me. These boys needed to relearn algebra before moving on to geometry! I imagined their intellectual abilities were OK but their self-esteem had taken a beating. At least making this assumption gave me hope. I had only a one-year contract. I knew I could not rescue them from this educational abyss, but I resolved to try!

What a thrill at year's end! Every member of 10E passed the statewide geometry exam. For some, this was their only success. Almost all of them ceased their formal schooling that year.

How did we do it? Refusing to collude with their conviction that maths was beyond them, I demanded they respect every moment spent in class. Realizing my belief in them was unshakable, they erected roadblocks to their learning. These obstacles revealed not only their ways of not learning but what had to happen for them to understand geometry.

Their blank stares and deadened affect taught me I should first help them discover mathematical principles. I thought this would be easy. They slept in rectangular beds, intuitively knew the shortest distance between two points is a straight line, could hit balls within parallel lines painted on a tennis court, and in PT regularly *circled* the cricket *oval*.

However, for learning to occur, they needed to be disciplined thinkers. That meant first becoming disciplined people. Achieving this depended on treating each other with respect. So, we instituted guidelines, which switched any negative comment about anything into praising whoever was willing to reveal his ignorance. Our slogan became "It is brave and smart to admit what you don't know." They were already brilliant at being bewildered!

Once these classroom norms were in place, we turned to the unlearned algebra. Starting with the basics, I tried to activate their mathematical curiosity, constantly looking for a chink in their intellectual armor. One morning a boy's eyes began to light up as if he were on the verge of grasping something new! I focused solely on him. Every time he gave off a cue of recognition, I went down the path his inquisitive looks suggested might be fruitful. Suddenly, he got it. I asked him to tell everyone what he had just figured out.

This was fresh in his mind. He knew what had made it difficult to understand and could talk in ways his peers could comprehend. Also, explaining it helped consolidate his own learning. I encouraged him to keep teaching until three others had taken in the lesson. Eager to make him look good, the whole class listened intently. Soon, several others had caught on. I then asked those who had got it to go desk by desk and tutor the rest of the boys.

This became our daily modus operandi. I would take an issue and teach my heart out until one student showed a glimmer of curiosity. Once the lesson sunk in, that boy shared his insights with the class, and we then tumbled into our organic tutoring pattern. We kept going until everyone understood. No shame was attached to being slow. Curiously, it was not the same boys that grasped the lesson of the hour. Soon, everyone had experienced being that day's algebra hero. This built an infectious spirit. To my surprise, without my ever suggesting it, these boys started helping each other after school. That accelerated their learning.

Eventually, peer tutoring became the norm in most high schools. But it certainly was not a known practice in the backwaters of Australian schooling when I was 20. Meanwhile, less and less was required of me. The students were doing most of the teaching. And never again did I have to speak to them about the virtues of learning.

Some issues were beyond my grasp. An example was how to communicate that one divided by zero is infinity. Fortunately, the school principal was a great math teacher. When stumped, I paid him a visit. "Kids need to *see* an abstract idea before learning the mathematics," he said. "Take two buckets to class, one filled with water, one empty, and a cup without a bottom. Ask a boy to transfer the water from the full to the empty bucket using the bottomless cup. He will refuse! Pressure others to do it. Keep insisting until they are in full-blown rebellion. As their excitement about your foolishness peaks, ask them why they won't do the task. They will protest and complain 'because it will take forever!' Then say 'this is what happens when you try to divide anything by zero. It takes forever. That's infinity!' Such approaches work wonders with our lads."

Only after rudimentary algebra was in place did I approach geometry. Hence, their midyear results were atrocious. I received no reprimand. No one had any expectations of 10E! I decided to stay the course with them. I knew this was a huge gamble, but other options were equally pointless.

When we began geometry, months later than the syllabus required, the students were motivated not by maths, which was zero, but in their belief that they could learn it. For them, this had become an exercise in building self-esteem. It was a joint enterprise. Any boy's failure to learn was seen as a reflection on them all. And anyone's mastery was celebrated as a shared success.

I loved the hours we spent in class. Their responsiveness led me to be more outrageous in both my mathematical demonstrations and my demands on them. They reciprocated.

On April Fools' Day, while arranging an experiment for a science class, I saw a rubber snake curled up near my feet. I paid it no heed until the boys' disappointment about my ignoring their prank became a distraction. When no one was expecting it, I picked up the snake and flung it at one of them. The whole class cheered.

Surprise! Surprise! In cahoots with 10E, my science students had hatched a plot. Later, with my geometry boys, I found another snake stashed in the supply closet. I picked it up and dumped it on my desk. It was huge compared with the one in my earlier class. I moaned, "Guys, I've already had the rubber snake routine today, where's your originality!"

There was an eerie hush in the room. Then came a yell, "Sir, it moved! The snake moved!"

Seeing only a lifeless blob on my desk, I said, "Fake snakes don't move! Give me a break!"

Determined to prove my point, I pinched the snake's tail. It reared up, its head right in front of my nose, fangs poised, ready to strike. I was panic-stricken. Eleven of the world's 15 most deadly snakes are indigenous to Australia! I didn't recognize this one. And for seconds fear held me in its grip. The boys roared with delight. I collapsed into a chair, sweating profusely.

"Gotcha, sir! We gotcha a beauty!"

I watched the snake slither to the back of the room, where a boy wrapped it around his chest. It was his pet.

10E never cracked a book that day. The whole period was spent telling snake stories.

I loved the outrageous things 10E and I did. We energized each other. Nearing year's end, I asked them to memorize theorems they could not reason from first principles. Surprisingly, they did this. Enough math logic had sunk in that some rote learning really increased their comprehension!

What I value most about that year is the education given to me by those boys who had been discarded by the school system. Whenever I see a snake now, I think of 10E, and I give thanks for the following things I learned under their tutelage:

- Classrooms exist to foster self-esteem.
- Understanding grows as learners access their own self-educator.
- Everyone has learning impediments that cause self-doubt.
- Our inadequacies are gateways to discovering what we do not know.
- Treating ignorance as an ally, instead of an alien, normalizes the aberrant.
- The best teachers are our fellow learners.
- Being in supportive settings helps when we are confronting tough lessons.
- We can only start where we are, not where others think we ought to be.[1]
- Insight is presaged by letting go of previous thoughts and feelings.
- Our limitations contain the key to unlocking what keeps us in an unknowing state.[2]

BELIEVING BREEDS ABUNDANCE

It is hard for kids to be around adults who see them as uneducable. These warehoused boys had little breathing room. For them, sport was the most wholesome part of any day. That physical release, plus the ties they shared due to their collective marginalization, probably saved their sanity. So, they and I were startled as their faith in the learning process grew. Despite their squashed spirits, they were still able to believe in themselves and each other.

Is it sacrilegious to use the words *faith* and *belief* in such a psychosocial manner? Although these concepts are primarily human processes, for generations they were locked in philosophical and theological enclaves, having been given spiritual or religious significances. In general, apart from refrains like "I believe only what I can see," standard discourse has repetitively shoved faith and belief into metaphysical closets. So sequestered, these concepts get given almost divine qualities. Then dogma tends to take over, resulting in moral imperatives about what one should believe and what can legitimately be called faith!

Belief is primarily a secular matter. Its relevance to shared learning shown by my 10E boys was well exemplified a decade later in the medical domain.

In the 1970s, Dr. Alexander Leaf, a respected scientist, discovered a surprising thing about beliefs. This Harvard physician set out to understand an anomaly about aging: why do people in some remote parts of the world age differently from those in populated areas? He found places in isolated regions of Pakistan, Georgia, the Southern Andes, etc., where a significant proportion of the aged were very healthy. In one small Andean area, for example, 1 percent of the population was over 100.[3] That was 300 times the rate in the USA and Japan.[4] In another region, people thought aging made them stronger. Hence, if an urgent message had to be sent among villages via runners, the job was given to men over 60. Why? Because they could easily outpace and outdistance the twenty-somethings! In these spots, degenerative diseases were rare. The elderly were hardly ever ill and had normal blood pressure, superb lung capacity, and good heart rates.

What accounted for this level of health and longevity? Was it linked to climate, diet, genetics, or lifestyle? Leaf tested the classic hypotheses, and some findings matched expectations. Low-fat, low-caloric diets helped, as did an active lifestyle. But that did not explain his overall observations.

Having studied the standard aging indicators using all the available medical tests of the era, he set that data aside and tried to look with fresh eyes. Then he noticed something unorthodox. *All these remote societies had a collective belief that aging was an enabling, not a degenerative process.* For them, midlife was a time of recalibration, not the start of a decline. And as people grew older, their communities treated them as being both wiser and more useful.[5]

Leaf left us with a provocative proposition: that *individual functioning*, even at the level of biology, might be wed to how *a whole community reasons and to its collective beliefs.*

Before the body, heart, mind, and spirit were segmented, people undoubtedly presumed that health was tied to what was occurring in all of one's being. However, the idea of communal beliefs directly impacting one's biology is counterintuitive in a world that seeks to explain behavior in terms of DNA and the genome. Leaf's notion is anecdotally plausible. It is logical that people living in war-torn lands would fall asleep anxious about what tomorrow might bring. It is equally likely that citizens feel sustained when love and mutual caretaking radiate through a society, even though many of them might not be direct beneficiaries of that generosity. Leaf's findings are in accord with what "being part of a universe" implies. The word *uni-verse* means *everything is interconnected*! If injurious chemicals are released into waterways, that toxicity is likely to enter the food chain. Likewise, communal socioemotional support and shared beliefs about the value of all creatures would get infused into a society's substrata. Old philosophies accepted this idea, as do many current ecological and social scientists.

A study in Roseto, Pennsylvania, made similar discoveries. From the Great Depression through the 1950s, this close-knit immigrant community had lower rates of heart disease than those in its surrounds. During the 1960s, the bonds among Roseto residents altered. Joining what was becoming the American dream, they moved from multigenerational to single-family dwellings. As valued former ties weakened, their rates of heart disease increased. Within 20 years, they were less healthy than those living in the communities that had been used as former comparison groups. As belief in mutual caretaking shrunk, their health deteriorated.[6] Alas, progress in one domain was being matched by a decline in another life arena!

Upon constructing cancer support groups, LeShan also learned the power of mutuality. He found that shared experiences had a substantial impact on the recovery and longevity of those with life-threatening illness. All members were dealing with the same issue— for example, women being treated for breast cancer. Because they intuited what each other was experiencing, there was little need to discuss their illnesses. That led them to address other things of import. Everyone had lost all illusions about their invincibility. Each person was grieving, automatically causing them to bond.

Previously held presumptions were shed, as they jointly built new beliefs based on the reality that each person's physical and emotional vulnerabilities would never vanish. These beliefs were grounded mainly on shared aspirations such as affirming they could do things that in the past they had lacked the courage to try. Examples were skydiving and initiating actions to assist people at greater risk than them. They were not focused on succeeding, only on finding the strength to begin something new. Because their beliefs were collective, these groups learned that jointly they were

58

stronger than the sum of their individual energies.

Building mutual emotional strength helped their healing. In the language of this book, the abundance they enjoyed resulted from creating shared beliefs, grounded on their own truths.[7] These findings illustrate that networks of mutual support and a common acceptance of values enhancing wellness and learning lead to a special form of abundance.

In the above arenas, abundance is tied to the collective and not to individuals. My 10E boys did not strive to be the best and were determined not to leave behind any failing peer. They dwelt on mutual success. In the Leaf studies, longevity was not a goal. Health was a mere byproduct. Their belief was in a value they jointly agreed to reinforce. The same was the case with the Roseto community and the LeShan cancer support groups.

Success measured by outcomes is a tough metric. When the aspiration is a way of being, then a triumph can be a fleeting soul-filled moment. Also, when abundance was experienced, scarcity was always in the shadows. Members of Roseto unknowingly traded abundance for more salubrious quarters and for a scarcity of a different kind. They wandered away from beliefs that had sustained them. Striving for more lavishness was costly in a noneconomic way. Leaf's people did not fight against anything. They accepted scarcity's ultimate dictum, that death is always nearby. The cancer support group members knew they would never be cancer free. For them, longevity was trivial in contrast with living each day, each week, each month as fully as possible.

A LEARNING EXTRAVAGANZA

During the 20th century, intellectual and industrial breakthroughs were astronomical. Communications advanced from crystal sets to machines facilitating millions of simultaneous person-to-person connections. Information once stored in libraries became digitally accessible. Cars, high-speed trains, and planes became normative. And we learned that our collective ignorance is much larger than our aggregated knowledge. This has led us to explore learning how to learn, to ask whether things seen as factual are valid, and to contemplate if convictions considered rock-solid are more than illusions-of-convenience. The above, plus two world wars, the Great Depression, the Holocaust, environmental degradation, and nuclear weapons show that this era has been full of both abundances and scarcities.

Basic learning is easy to grasp. Infants mimic the sounds of caretakers. Chicks tune in to chirps heralding danger. Foals spring to their feet as their infant muscles cry out to be stretched. Ducklings swim when coaxed into the water. But learning about learning?

Many adults today wonder whether what they learned as children was anything more than a reflection of established cultural mores and prevailing educational practices. Painfully, schooling can advance or shrink comprehension! That observation had led us to question whether so-called knowledge is anything more that an artifact of the methodologies used to investigate the unknown!

Educational enterprises have repetitively demonstrated several robust findings. Most information imparted in classrooms can be taught via videos and animated digital chalkboards.[8] The unschooled when given access to computers, without having an instructor can jointly turn unfamiliar machines into teaching devices.[9] Also noninvasive, group-based, discovery principles and self-led learning environments do produce quality learning.[10]

While depending on computer-assisted instruction has drawbacks, such as children spending too much time peering at screens, what is considered basic knowledge is now fully available on the Internet. But that has produced another concern, how to develop creativity, critical thinking, collaboration and mutual problem-solving skills.[11] Fortunately, there are institutions like Montessori and Waldorf that addressed these themes long ago.

They base education on constructing rather than instructing, on viewing everything from multiple vantage points, on generating insights rather than memorizing facts, on finding one's own voice, on establishing a moral core, on connecting with people who think differently, on acquiring cultural sensitivities, and on artistic expression.[12] These processes are present in the best educational settings. However, they have yet to reach under-resourced and rigidly structured school systems.

There are many psychically demanding forms of learning: how to make wholesome, relational adjustments at various stages of partnering; how to manage the ambiguities upon receiving a life-threatening diagnosis; how to genuinely accept one's own flaws; how to accept unwanted advice; how to age gracefully; how to live with soul-shattering grief. This type of learning requires us to remain consistently on the cusp of our ignorance, which is where authentic learning occurs. Even acknowledging, let alone dwelling on our unknowingness is anxiety provoking. Justifiably, we close down to evade such troublesome feelings. That usually leads to our not allocating the time needed for the potential lessons to adequately germinate.

In the above, the scarcity-abundance relationship is evident, as are the faith and beliefs of people often laboring under or learning how to live within difficult conditions.

A big challenge remains. Functional relationships are necessary to convert knowledge into action. Creating essentials like food, health care, and public transportation relies on the collaboration of many people, groups, and organizations. This means humans are continuously learning to co-labor with diverse peoples, to synchronize the thoughts and feelings of multiple constituencies and to appropriately link human capacities with machine technologies. Also learning is not just cerebral. It is also interactive, visual, auditory and tactile. A good example is the finger dexterity of doctors doing robotic surgery, at the same time managing the complexities of group-based collaboration and multi-faceted person-machine interfaces.

Building high levels of emotional functionality among multiple and diverse constituencies, although rewarding, is also taxing. Obviously, a lot of these skills already exist. We would not have reached our current state unless that was the case. However, we can readily see that the type of learning-how-to-learn ahead of us is still embryonic. Our collective belief in the future-that-will-be is still to evolve, as is our faith in each other, our environment and the cosmos. As these develop, so will the abundance-scarcity dynamic that has brought us this far in a few short millennia.

A *BUDDHIST* CONTRIBUTION TO LEARNING ABOUT ABUNDANCE

Both discovery learning and psychosocial healing help align disparate concepts, harmonize discordant energies, and integrate divisive agendas. They are both similar to the *Taoist* prinς enabling possibility to emerge from the improbable. Giving shapς the formless requires belief in the transformational process and that the new will amplify and not diminish what previously existed.

Healing is a learning process. And learning is a healing process. Pain and ignorance are signs of a problematic instability. That disequilibrium is a catalyst for change. The diagnostic treatment or the educational phase is the intervention. In the case of healing, the result may be recovery or the acceptance of a chronic condition. In the learning arena, the result may be new understandings or the acceptance of a newly recognized ignorance.

Restoration of the human body and the generation of insight are based on the same *yin-yang* dynamic found in biological reparation, all of which are highly dependent on faith and belief. Were it not for the contributions of learning, healing, faith, and belief, the abundance-scarcity phenomenon would be vacuous.

Perhaps the best known and most skilled scholar to labor in the learning-healing domain was Siddhartha Gautama, born around 500 BCE into a regal family residing in the Himalayan foothills of Nepal. Approaching maturity, he exited his privileged cloister and witnessed the communal agonies of the populace. This fall from innocence flung him off his princely trajectory. According to the legendary accounts, this man now known as the *Buddha* left behind everything. As a homeless wanderer, he pursued the meditative arts and the self-mortification practices of local indigents. In time, he grew disillusioned with this path.

Recognizing how much suffering was caused by the grind of daily life, he started studying the human condition, searching for ways to alleviate the people's psychic pains. Upon devising methodologies that could be a healing force he became an itinerant teacher. Aided by his followers, Gautama spent his last 45 years offering assistance to those ready and open to receiving his message.[13]

His insights were passed on via the oral tradition. Initially, the monks memorized and recited his teachings, giving them a repetitious and poetic structure that was sung or chanted. That made them easy to preserve and pass along. A body of written work was created 400 years after his death at age 80.[14] The record is in Pali, Sanskrit, or one of the Prakrits, all languages unfamiliar to Siddhartha. Because the oral cannon was adjusted to fit the changing times and diverse cultures, the *Buddha's* ideas morphed into dogmas that were managed by disciples who struggled with multiple schisms. However, scholars have traced the main doctrinal modifications and created an integrated knowledge base. Centuries later, *Buddhism's* center shifted to China and Tibet, so these teachings are also enshrined in other Asian languages.[15]

The Gautama family resided in a region with established cities that was later fused with the Mauryan Empire, a dominant sociopolitical superstructure.[16] For ages, the societal fabric had reinforced the caste structure that prescribed the attributes individuals were to adopt. Change was mostly resisted.[17]

Gautama saw that the elites exploited the underpaid and then disparaged these same people for being impoverished. He set out to dismantle these hierarchical practices. He wanted sociopolitical and moral judgments to be based on what people contributed to society, not the status society forced upon them. The *Buddha* and his followers knew that people at all levels needed to become aware of their own and others' condition, along with the bedrock values on which their realities were based.[18]

Relying solely on the resources he could excavate from his own inner being, Gautama was a sophisticated sociopsychological investigator and reformer. He wanted humanity to alter how it conceptualized life. So, he set out to create new knowledge and to test the relevance of his insights in the hurly burly of regular life. Then he started educating people about the self-generating cycles of suffering that kept them locked in drudgery. This was a visionary enterprise of enormous proportions. Over the next 2,500 years, the *Buddha's* followers contributed many insights about humans' minds and emotions, along with the problems of societies at large.

For my purposes here, I will turn to one thought expressed by a contemporary *Buddhist* writer that is especially relevant to the abundance-scarcity-faith-belief-learning-healing nexus.[19]

Because we tend to think of objects, creatures, people, ecosystems, planets, etc., as discrete entities, we fail to notice how interdependent they are with all other things. It is well known that at the macro level everything is nested within larger systems and that inside the microscopic there is a universe of structures and dynamics. Yet we often act as if we are discrete entities and fail to attend to our inter-being-ness.

When looking at an object or a life-form, it is hard to attend to the many ways it is linked to the rest of the one universal organism of which all things, us included, are a part. Failing to see this, we erroneously ascribe attributes to those elements that we split off from the whole. This form of functioning leads to our noticing boundaries that don't exist except in our minds. These false delineations limit the influence we have when interacting with other so-called entities, thereby unwittingly creating scarcity. But this dearth is an illusion! It is a byproduct of false thinking, as *Buddhists* consistently remind us.

By natural processes, our awareness of abundance may be scant.

When the price of bread increases, do we grumble about rising costs, or do we celebrate all the hands that labor to nourish us? How different life would be if every day we thought about all who contributed to the bread we eat: the farmers who till the soil, plant the seeds, tend the field and gather the crops; the workers who grind the grain, package, and ship it to market; the bakers who knead the dough, light the fire, and regulate the oven's temperature; the people who make the plows, build the trucks to transport the grain, and generate the electricity to light the bakery.

Then there are the overlooked but miraculous ways showers, sun, and soil transform a seed into a plant that gives forth thousands of new seeds. Each grain carries the presence of the clouds. Without clouds, there would be no rain. Without rain, there would be no plants. Without plants, there would be no wheat, barley, oats, or quinoa, and hence no bread. Each grain also has imprints of the soil made fertile by phosphorous, potassium, and nitrogen, plus microorganisms like fungi, bacteria, and algae, along with the ants, worms, etc.

The bread is also a container of the sun's energies. Without the sun, no electromagnetic radiation producing photosynthesis would exist. Without photosynthesis, there would not be any plants or carbohydrates. If the only thing we ate today was a single slice of bread, we may feel physically undernourished. Yet if before eating we reflected on the abundance created by the interdependencies of rain, earth, cosmic energy, human labor, and the ingenuity that harnessed electricity, created machines, built viable marketplaces and so forth, our hearts would be full of gratitude for even a handful of crumbs.

There is another hidden form of abundance. It is evidenced by how much we believe in what nature provides and what micro-

critters as well as humans do to keep us alive every s
Virtually all humans each day knowingly or unknowingly believ
the competence, kindness, and faithfulness of hundreds of people
who enable us to have the food we need. We count on them to do
their job with integrity.

Equally impressive is our belief we have in all the people who
make functional the systems we rely upon, garbage collectors,
teachers, bus drivers, health care professionals, police, AI, and so
forth. Somehow, collectively, we have learned that almost all
people, while doing their assigned tasks, are trustworthy and that it
is in everyone's interest to rely on their dependability. The
abundance of nature's gifts is irrefutable. Equally impressive are the
beliefs that members of all nations give expression to every minute
of every single day.

This degree of self-generating abundance, this expansive
balance of *just-enoughness* and *not-too-muchness* is stunning. Even
in moments when we feel the pangs of scarcity, the belief we have
in life itself is abundant beyond measure. Learning to accept these
realities is healing.

SUMMARY

Learning and healing are about building and restoring.
Constructing a life entails two forms of discovery. One occurs
within constraints. Another takes place in the open spaces where it
is possible to experiment without fear of failure. Healing is a
mobilization of nature's renewal systems. But if repair is not
possible, the remedial work is learning how to build new ways for
the body to function. When building a home or seeking help to
reconstruct our lives, we choose to believe that the contractor or the

.tion and create a spaciousness sufficient
.hed. If we added together all the times we
Jbs that sustain us, we would realize that the
we have is our collective belief. Here is a
at this chapter addressed:

- ,g occurs on the cusp of our ignorance.
- Disc vering new things is a risky business!
- Wanting more-than-enough increases our sense of scarcity.
- Collective belief in abundance transports us from a *having* to a *being* state.
- Wisdom appears when superfluous facts fade away.
- Now is always the perfect moment to learn what we most need to know.
- Learning is healing, and healing is awash with learning.
- It takes a leap of faith to give form to the formless.
- Daily we rely upon the millions of creatures taking up residence in our bodies.
- Life depends upon a good measure of both abundance and scarcity.

CHAPTER 5

GENEROSITY AMIDST DEMORALIZING SCARCITY

Generosity is like a river, always flowing, eternally present.[1]

Nature is abundantly generous. Humans are filled with that same generosity. When kind-heartedness is absent, some blockage is creating that scarcity.

Generosity is a faithful contributor to the abundance-scarcity dynamic. Is it a thing, like a bucket? Is it an art, like music? Is it a force, like gravity? Is it an essential, like air? Is it a luxury, like ice cream? Is it a necessity, like rice? Is it a foundation, like the earth? It is all those things and much more! Generosity may not be something we see or fully understand. However, we know generosity because it is a part of everyone, perpetually sustaining us. This vast, indescribable sensation enters our beings via those elegant gateways, trust, faith, and belief.

Generosity is one of those psychosocial energies affixed to human experiences. Yet it is even more lavishly expressed by nature. It is in a raindrop kissing a dried-out leaf, in a bird's song peacefully punctuating a silence, in a sunray peering through a cloud, in a newborn bringing to the world a fresh infusion of adorability.

This chapter opens a new phase of the abundance discovery process.

It starts with a story that seemed encased in extreme scarcity and almost zero generosity but ended with an overwhelming sense of abundance. In this event are three seminal themes: (1) Even in the midst of derailed human systems there are self-correcting forces flowing from the generous souls on the bus, on the factory floor, on the street. (2) When a psychological sense of scarcity dominates a landscape, underground streams of generosity start working their way to the surface. (3) Even in oppressive settings, safe havens organically surface.

The discussion about the above themes is followed by an exploration of a difficult process that almost every one of us still has to master. All around us are people who we do not like, who do things we dislike. We then use our pent-up disdain for our dislikes to justify having prejudicial feelings toward them. However, the mere act of looking at their actions through a lens of generosity begins to produce a psychological sense of abundance.

The chapter ends with an exhortation to readers from India and China, two peoples who are still struggling to release themselves from long-standing enmities. The Indian concepts of *karma* and *dharma* are used as a bridge between generosity and abundance and between the two philosophies, *Hinduism* and *Taoism* that have long grounded the peoples of these nations.

DEPORTATION

The letter sent shivers down my spine. The Immigration and Naturalization Service (INS, now known as Homeland Security) was informing me I was to be deported. I had no idea why. For years, *INS-phobia* had been a regular, but unwanted, guest. Like many other outsiders, I lived on a razor's edge. My work visa was renewed annually. Each November my employer certified they still wanted my services. Like clockwork, the following February, I was granted a new visa. This had been working fine, and I came to appreciate the predictability of this process.

I raced to the INS, seeking help. That led to the following conversation: "What went wrong? *You are an illegal alien!* Why? *You broke the law!* What law? *We can't tell you!* Why not? *Because you are an illegal alien!*" I did not know whether to weep or go into a rage!

An advisor helped piece together my transgression. In September I began a new job in a different state, not knowing I needed INS approval to relocate. My visa was stamped "valid until Feb." I followed the stipulated ritual and reapplied in November. In January, the INS said my visa was not renewed and began using words like *illegal*, *alien*, and *deportation*.

I returned to the INS. Again, the exchange was bizarre. "Is there something wrong with my current visa? *You don't have a current visa!* It says 'valid until Feb!' *It expired when you moved to Pennsylvania!* A visa is linked to a particular state? *You broke the law when you left Maryland!* How was I to know this? *It is coded in the visa numbers!* That information is in this set of numbers that look random to me? *Yes!* Can I please see a copy of the regulations? *Sorry, honey, I can't do that!* Why not? *Because you're an illegal!*" My humanity had been expunged! To officialdom, I was now not just an *alien* but an *illegal* one. How exotic!

Expressing my despair, I threw my arms in the air, shrugging my leaden shoulders.

Suddenly, everything changed. This same lady, pulling herself close to me, patted my sweating hand, and in a motherly manner mouthed, "Hire an immigration lawyer!"

"What are you saying?" I asked, calmed by her quiet, caring affect.

"I am whispering because I am not allowed to tell you this: hire an immigration lawyer!"

I looked into her face. It was awash with kindness. I thanked her and left.

What a moment! An officer in a governmental unit designed to cull the undesirables had compassionately offered me, a complete stranger, some much-needed guidance. That gift altered my ordeal. And due to her generosity, the rigidity of my stiffened heart lessened.

My newly found lawyer painted this picture for me. "When you apply for a visa, your case is reviewed to make sure you are complying with the regulations. If not, you must leave the country or you will be deported. However, officials handling these cases can sniff an injustice. They do not believe in the system they must implement and know how to get around situations like this."

Having concocted an intriguing plan to help get me out of my legal bind, he said, "Please follow my instructions precisely. We will be relying on good people inside the bureaucracy who understand what we are doing. They will turn a blind eye at every point along the way but will insist you obey the law. We are working a legal loophole. I will resubmit your visa application to Office A. They will approve it and right away give me a copy of your visa renewal. That same day Office A will send your file to Office B, which will stamp it 'illegal alien' and start deportation procedures. As soon as I receive your papers, I will call you. Go to the airport immediately and buy a one-way ticket for the first available flight to London. I will come to the airport and give you a copy of your newly approved visa papers. I will then head to Office B. Once your flight is airborne, I'll give them a copy of your London ticket and tell them there is no need to serve you deportation papers since you have already left. That will stop them from ever preparing those incriminating documents!"

"OK," I said. "That gets me out of the country. What then?"

"When you get to London, go to the United States Embassy and give them your newly approved visa papers. They will ask you several carefully worded questions. One will deal with deportation. They will not ask if you have broken any immigration laws, been designated an illegal alien, or been rejected for a visa. They will ask if you have ever been served deportation papers. Because you were never *served* them, you can truthfully say 'no.' Do **NOT** volunteer any information about anything you are not asked. These officials will not try to trap you. Since in all other regards your record is unblemished, they will grant you a new visa. This is strange, but at that moment, all previous transgressions are automatically removed from your record. You can then buy a ticket and return to the USA."

Putting my faith in my lawyer's counsel, I obeyed his directions. It worked. Through a long stream of events, every person was truly collaborative. Later when I applied for permanent resident status, it was granted. My former visa kafuffles were never mentioned!

Encountering the INS was painful. Yet throughout, I experienced the kindness of strangers who helped me, not because of who I was, but because of who they were. Their spirits were stronger than the strictures prescribed by the regulations they had to implement! That year the scales fell from my eyes. Never again did I return to my former ways of seeing.

Many a door is closed to us unless an insider opens it. The excluded can only knock and wait to be invited in. When the latch is released, we enter on their terms, not ours. Our entrée is always due to their largess, not our worthiness, irrespective of what we have to offer. It is wise to remember that we are barred because those with the key are unable or unwilling to open the door. That reveals more about the condition of the key holders than the entry seekers. When the door is unbolted, we are extended the hospitality the insiders can mobilize. This is true of homes we wish to enter, of nations we wish to reside in, of hearts we wish to connect with more fully. Yet after feeling rejected, we often discover that a kind soul has left unlocked for us a back door located at the end of an unlit, unpretentious path through the shadows.

KINDNESS WITHIN A HEARTLESS SYSTEM

An impressive network of individuals saved me from a downward spiral: the INS official who suggested I seek legal help, my lawyer, visa processors colluding to circumvent a contorted law, officers in London's US Embassy. With no direct ties to those operating across vast oceans, every person was a cog in a covert scheme. This was a unique episode in my life. Yet on any day these civil servants probably helped hundreds of people in similar ways.

How did these agents feel about their actions? Since releasing a portion of the generosity located in one's inner reservoir provides its own rewards to the giver, they undoubtedly felt fine. However, none of them would ever know the consequences of their actions. So, in each case, they had to decide whether to implement the rogue immigration subculture or apply the rules explicated by the legal system. It is surprising but wonderful that such generosity existed within a unit mandated to be merciless as it rounded up and disposed of the wrongdoers.

This covert INS system echoes the Underground Railroad, that collaborative network of abolitionists, which helped runaway slaves escape the clutches of slave owners. It also resembles the network of citizens in sanctuary cities working to prevent the deportation of families who, without legal papers, came to places like Philadelphia in search of a safe haven. These women, men, and children are desperate not to be returned to the political vulnerability, economic enslavement, and troubled contexts from which they had fled.

Initially I had been enraged by the INS, so their final gift to me was reparative. However, it is troubling that systems built to do valuable things end up developing perversities. Clearly what happened to me and to probably hundreds of thousands in similar situations that year was not designed to trick people into breaking invisible and unknowable laws. The INS was tough even for an English speaker with a skin color and a name unlikely to set off the security system's alarms. I cannot imagine encountering this uncongenial institution with none of these privileging criteria!

Yet, with the exception of the all-pervasive devastations associated with slavery and the brutal displacements of the indigenous peoples from their lands, this country is made up of immigrants and refugees. So, decade after decade, the processes of migration have worked effectively for millions. Given the scarcity traps, that means a huge amount of kindness was extended to many people. That was made possible by systems that did work effectively, undoubtedly lubricated by the same form of generosity that saved me from the abyss.

This deportation story is also similar to the discussions in a previous chapter about medical logics. While we may have 1 percent of our cells failing to function in the correct way, thereby making us ill, 99 percent of our body is doing just fine. So, the anxiety-produced scarcity I endured for a short period was tiny compared with the situations that worked well. Again, this raises the question of where we choose to keep our focus. On the scarcities, the symptoms of a pathology that are few in number, or on the abundance of healthy functionality?

How often am I treated with the generosity of the lady in the INS office who whispered caringly the secret code that helped unlock my bind, or the behind-the-scene government officials who invent ways to circumvent unjust laws, or those who assist innocents caught in an impossible conundrum. My answer is many times a day. Even though I do not know them and will never have the opportunity to thank them, they silently and continuously help to sustain people's psychological sense of abundance.

BUILDING NEW PSYCHOSOCIAL BONDS

How many times have I been told explicitly I am to be deported? From my country of residence, only once! However, organizations regularly dismiss employees, exclude from the inner circle people entitled to a seat at a decision-making table, and shun those who hold values disagreeable to the establishment. These too are deportations! This has happened to me many times. And regrettably, I too have deported people from one setting or another.

At a much deeper level, though, I regularly act as a deportation agent. I don't mean orchestrating an ousting from a country or a workplace. I am referring to deporting parts of myself I want banished. Dumping unwanted emotions into someone else's lap. Flinging to the furthest reaches those thoughts I consider ridiculous. Grinding into dust impulses I suspect might be harmful. Extruding germs from my body that are making me ill. Some of these actions may seem justifiable. However, this means the junk I do not want in my own backyard gets transferred to some other place. These are, after all, my emotions, my thoughts, my impulses and my germs.

Disowning them merely relocates to another world what I want extruded.

When looking closely at this behavior, it is obvious that the deportation process is directed primarily at the deportee, at the things being deported. Of much greater import is what does the actual deportation process do to the one doing the deporting? What I now recognize is that when I try to deport anything, especially the ugly and inherently dislikeable bits of my nature, my spirit shrinks a bit more. And when I bring back into my being what I have previously jettisoned, my interiority grows larger and begins to function as my spirit's sanctuary.

Our Higher Self calls us to love every part of us, even those things about ourselves we do not like! When we fail to do that, we are acting as our own deporting agent. Over the years, I deported many parts of myself to other places, and it has taken half my life to regather them. No external body did that deporting of me. I did it to myself. By so doing, I was the creator of my own psychological sense of scarcity. Fortunately, that means I can be the author of my own psychological sense of abundance by being fully mindful of what is migrating into me and by not deporting the things that truly belong to me, be they good or bad.

Every day we face a choice. Will we treat those we encounter with a spirit of generosity or marginalize them? At day's end, if we have engaged in marginalizing, how do we feel about the people we ostracized and the self who did the ostracizing? If we have been kindly in all our encounters, what is our spirit's condition as we settle into slumber?

In 2016, the USA held an extremely polarizing presidential election. The two major candidates worked relentlessly to characterize his or her opponent as an awful and incompetent human being. The sociopolitical air was filled with fear and hatred. The electorate, fueled by a commercial and social media frenzy warped by fake news, exacerbated the situation. Virtually all the nation's potential voters were engaged in demeaning the candidate they wanted to lose. They also sprayed unconscionable amounts of venom upon their neighbors, workmates, and family members who held views different from their own. The emotional climate in the country was putrid. Immediately following the election, a dark pall of depression hung heavy over the land. Even those happy with the candidate who won seemed off-kilter, out-of-sorts, miserable.

In my view, this nation had created for itself one of the most complex challenges since the Civil War of the 1860s and the Great Depression of the 1930s. In the ensuing weeks, I was in gatherings with many people, graduate students in the USA and India, superintendents of public schools in the Philadelphia region, and colleagues of all stripes. At some point in our exchanges, they asked for my advice on how to deal with the aftermath of the election, especially because the reverberations were negatively impacting them and the people around them. This is what I thought and ultimately chose to say, after reminding all listeners that I am not an American citizen and hence am speaking as an outsider, as a guest in the USA.

The biggest problem is not really visible and is not easy to discuss. Far more important than who won the election or the new government's political priorities, is what we have all done and are now doing to ourselves as individuals and as a nation. Speaking metaphorically, I think this extreme demeaning of others during this election has injected poison into every crevice of our beings. We thought that what we were doing was hurting our opponents. That undoubtedly was correct. But no matter where we sit on any political spectrum, that was minor in contrast to what we did to our fellow citizens and ourselves. We have collectively made ourselves into a whole nation of demeaning people with little capacity to stop ourselves or to help others from spreading the attendant emotional toxicity! I see only one way out of this morass. And it has to be done person by person. It will not be possible to address at a public policy level and no amount of psychotherapy will make a dent. This is the sole option, and fortunately it is available to all of us for free. The question is will we take on this task and do it faithfully, with integrity, for as long as is necessary, which may take several generations?

Our task now is to learn to love those we do not like or who do things we loathe. Many of us seem able and willing to love those we like. Loving those who share our values is good and should never be decreased. But the big question is can we learn to love those we despise! This dilemma is reminiscent of something a state commissioner of corrections in the USA once told me was the hardest part about the job of running the prison system. It was that every time he faced a convicted individual he had to accept the contempt he felt for what that person did without ever feeling contempt for him or her as a human being. That level of emotional sophistication is what we are now required to develop, to save ourselves, let alone to repair this nation's self-inflicted wounds.

This is what I think is the most important thing I can say to anyone who wants to discuss this topic. I am sure we all have someone in our larger family who does things we dislike, who takes postures thoroughly antithetical to our own, who gets under our skin. But when they are hungry, we feed them. When they are downtrodden, we hug them. When they are ill, we take care of them. And when they die, we bury them. To love is to embrace others with an open and accepting heart, no matter what. I am equally sure that if we all look at ourselves in the mirror for long enough, we will notice things about us we don't like: that ugly pimple, those unwanted emotions, that receding hairline, those aches that keep reappearing, that growing forgetfulness, and so forth. It is easy to love the parts of us that are adorable, but we are called to love all of ourselves, even the bits of us that we sometimes deride!

The response of most people to these words of mine is usually silence, with a composed recognition that I am saying to them something they already know.

If I am discussing this with students in a formal course, I ask them to look around the room and notice all the things their peers do, think, or feel that they like and those they dislike. Then I suggest they go person by person and tell each compatriot what the likes and dislikes were. I also request that they conclude each exchange by telling the other person that, "irrespective of my explicit dislikes, I commit to loving you, because in the final analysis, what I don't like about you says more about me than anything else." It amazes me how quickly these students, most of whom are in their twenties and thirties, jump up and full-heartedly respond to this invitation. The energy in the room is electric. I tend to do this toward the end of a class session. As they look to me for a closing statement, I usually remind them that the only truly redemptive force is love, which is freely gifted to everyone.

No matter what part of the world we live in, our race, our economic status, or our political positions, we all have within us a deep reservoir of generosity that is easy to access once it is uncorked. For most people, our own fountain of charitableness is blocked until some external catalyst or an inner crisis gives us a jolt that unleashes it.

It is surprising that generosity, which is thoroughly familiar to us and is as abundant as our very breath, is most of the time quite blocked. Ironically, lacking the natural flow of munificence from our inner wells, we tend to feel that others are inadequately generous toward us. We impatiently wait for them to sprinkle dewdrops of kindness upon us and wonder why this happens so infrequently. In reality, it is not other's generosity we crave most but permission to release our own.

Why do we fear our generosity? Probably because we suspect it has been repressed for so long it might emerge like a volcanic eruption and blow away everything we cherish. That is unlikely, of course, because nature has equipped us with easy to identify spigots that can modulate the flow. We are the authors of our own psychological sense of abundance and of scarcity. If we want to alter it, we can open wider or close down our generosity faucet.

For years I have been involved with graduate students in India, nowadays about 300 annually. One time all our hearts had been ripped apart by what had recently occurred in their country. I was at a loss about what to say to these Indian twenty-somethings who felt emotionally and intellectually crushed by the butchery created by some individuals who had lost their moorings. Wanting some guidance about how to handle the situation, I went to the Gandhi memorial and stood by the eternal flame lit in remembrance of the Mahatma.

Lost in thought, I tearfully had an imaginary conversation with Gandhi, asking him if he had any advice to offer me. The reply that formed in me was clear and strong: "Tell them what is in your heart."

The next day I shared with my students this inner chat with the Gandhi-inside-me and plowed headlong into the topic that was troubling us all. They were so attentive I chose to say what I was convinced Gandhi would have wanted me to pass along to them. One of the greatest challenges this generation of Indians faces is how to forge meaningful partnerships with the Chinese. The world needs Indians and Chinese to be good collaborators. Together they represent 40 percent of the world's population and will soon control 40 percent of the world's wealth. Yet they don't like each other in large part because their histories have blocked them from knowing one another as human beings.

If Gandhi were here today, I am convinced he would say to this generation of Indians: "Please figure out what you do and do not like about the Chinese and then learn to love them, despite your dislikes. All Asians are each other's brothers and sisters. Please return to your own philosophical roots and reclaim the best of your traditions."

I will turn now to a couple of the *Hindu* thoughts that shed light on abundance as they relate to the theme of generosity and the abundance big-heartedness creates.

INDIAN LOGOS

Two of that nation's most cherished concepts are *karma* and *dharma*. These are constructs Indian parents plant in an offspring's budding heart before its intellect is developed. Hence, they are ever present in most Indians' attitudes and beliefs.[2]

Karma signifies *action*. It is that force of nature that shapes, equips, and sustains each being's existence.[3] *Karma* is also the sum of the affect affixed to what one does and to what motivated that behavior. Its meaning changes when the context is altered or when an ascribing agent's agenda is modified. Noble or nefarious intent, along with the consequences of an outcome, get attached, like a sweet or pungent odor, to both the action and the doer of a deed.[4] The impact of *karma* can be direct or delayed. It metaphorically can stream into one or several settings, cause troublesome crosscurrents, divert drops to parched places, build a bog, or slake a swamp.[5] Basically, good *karma* is meritorious; bad *karma* accumulates demerits.[6] In the context of this chapter, *karma* can be thought of as increasing or decreasing generosity and its affiliate, the psychological sense of abundance.

Getting free of *karmic* constraints starts with accepting several things: that all sensations are tied to one's personal predispositions; that all experience is subjective; that overfiltering what is allowed to enter one's inner sanctum is self-limiting; that one's being is but a tiny portion of the *Universal Self*; that everyone is a cocreator of her or his essentiality.[7]

Indian philosophies assert that after a thing or being vanishes, it may reappear in a new biochemical structure, based in part on the quality of its *karma*.[8] This is easy to imagine at summer's end, watching a withering flower that will spring forth as beautiful as ever in a later season. But when applied to creatures living in an ashes-to-ashes, dust-to-dust cycle, it is hard to picture how we can cart with us our earned or ascribed *karma*, since our future existence is certain to be in a different context and in a fresh energy cocoon. Yet this seems a palatable idea when stripped of classic metaphysical accoutrements and viewed as part of nature's normal ways.

Karmic thinking implies we enter life with prior dispositions, kept in check by invisible, sociological, genetic, biological and spiritual boundaries. This inspires Indian parents to adopt flexible, patient, accepting approaches to most things, expecting that if something of import is inadequately dealt with it will cycle around again.[9] Irrespective of whether this is valid, it is a very generous way to parent and to befriend adversaries. And it augments abundance.

Dharma, the second foundational concept, given its broad etiological base, has many meanings.[10] The attributes of *dharma* have evolved over time and vary from holding and maintaining through to regulating change by not striving to regulate change. No definition is fully adequate. That said, colloquially, *dharma* signifies correct ways to live, the righteous path,[11] plus all the behaviors that advance individual, familial, and societal functionality.[12]

For Indians, forming relationships involves getting a sense of one another's *dharma*, the shaper of each person's behavior.[13] At the individual level, *dharma* is seen in one's disposition, acceptance of moral duties, desire to do the right thing, truthfulness, conformity to appropriate norms, etc. At the collective level, *dharma* is a moral anchor. However, because Indian integrity relies on *dharma*, which is highly relativistic, its meaning alters as contexts change. It is a shock absorber when relationships are whiplashed. It connects past, present, and future. It is a buffer during ethical clashes. It upholds revered traditions. It produces sufficient spaciousness for modernity and innovation to be incorporated within antiquity's boundaries.[14]

As with the Jungian union of light and shadow, *dharma* exists alongside its opposite, *adharma* (not *dharma*). When *adharma* is dominant in people, they are usually described as immoral, narcissistic, unlawful, egotistical.[15] Historically, the *dharma-adharma* dynamic placed both self and other into a social space, thereby giving people some stable societal referent points. Hence, problematically and prejudicially, *dharma-adharma* has been tied to identity tags like caste, gender, diet, religion, etc. Caste has been a deeply problematic force in India, but many who accept their lower caste tag provide communal services courageously, dutifully, and lawfully, which are strong *dharma* attributes.[16]

Indian ethics are often misunderstood due to the relativism of *dharma*. This can make some statements by Indians appear inadequately truthful, not because of what is said but because of what is omitted. It makes some decisions appear too easy to alter at a whim, too nebulous to rely on. However, the roominess of this relativism makes the Indian way of being graciously relational and requires them to be highly attuned to one another's emotions. It also helps sustain the abundant connections from which the mutuality among many diverse peoples is established. In short, Indians are wonderful friends, due in large part to *dharma*.[17] This gives a depth and sponginess to their relatedness that cushions and sustains their nation's vitality.

Do *dharma* and *karma* represent reality? Are these concepts valid? These topics are hotly debated by scholars. That is not our concern here. There is something of far greater import. *Dharma* and *karma* are so sociologically valuable to Indians that they continuously strive to ensure that these processes remain solidly embedded in their way of being.[18]

SUMMARY

These are the themes addressed in this chapter:

- Like a river, generosity flows without becoming depleted.
- Our very existence is dependent on the generosity of others.
- Kindness is present even in seemingly heartless systems.
- Generosity-filled safe havens exist in unexpected places.
- Our brokenness is tiny beside all that functions well.

- We are all constantly deporting or importing others from or into our emotional worlds.
- We always have a choice to be generous or mean-spirited.
- Learning how to love those we dislike is our emotional Mt. Everest.
- Generosity builds a psychological sense of abundance.
- *Karma* and *dharma* link generosity and abundance.

CHAPTER 6
GRATITUDE'S GIFTS

Our capacity for gratitude is one of nature's many gifts to us. This may seem a strange statement, since gratefulness is a human construct. However, the bountiful blossoms or delectable fruits released by plants and trees can be seen as expressing a form of appreciation for the water, fertilizers, and nutrients that sustain them. So it is with us. In the final analysis, all human thoughts, emotions, or actions are manifested via the biochemical vessels and mechanisms given to us.

The last chapter highlighted that generosity flows like a river, and even when blocked, underground streams find a way to reach distant destinations. Gratitude functions similarly. While analyzing my deportation experience, I used a phrase, the "psychological sense of abundance," which generosity greatly amplifies. Its close partner, gratitude, also makes unceasing contributions to the abundance wellsprings.

By the end of this chapter, we will have explored what I think are the five fundamental pillars of abundance: trust, faith, belief, generosity, and gratitude.

Again I start with a story, which might seem like a repeat of the generosity-grows-gratitude theme. However, there is a circuitous process that needs to be considered. Not only is gratitude a major response to generosity, gratitude contributes substantially to the actual generation of generosity. In short, gratitude and generosity are mutually causal.

I will examine gratitude at both the interpersonal and the intra-psychic levels.

This probe into gratitude and its links with generosity in general and abundance in particular includes a discussion of six themes: (1) gratitude and generosity cocreate each other; (2) conjoined, they are a potent amplifier of abundance; (3) generosity and gratitude are not usually outwardly visible but can be noticed by those who have cultivated a form of deep listening; (4) although not always recognized or acknowledged, streams of gratitude and streams of generosity are constantly flowing into and out of us; (5) when generosity is fully received it is a gift to both the recipient and the giver; (6) to adequately absorb the concept of gratitude, it helps to recognize that all elements of our life are dependent on the generosity of nature, without which we would not even exist.

This discussion of gratitude is punctuated with occasional thoughts that come from several ancient philosophical traditions.

PLANTING THE SELF IN FOREIGN SOIL

I began my 30-hour flight from my homeland, inhaling hope, exhaling anxiety. It was time to end my nomadism.[1] Having grown weary of looking for a place I could call home, I had decided to immerse myself in a job at a campus on the outskirts of Washington.

I had dreamed of buying a small place in a quaint crevice of DC but upon beginning my search realized all I could afford in the nation's capital was a one-car garage! I refocused and selected a community with tree-lined streets close to my university, which at springtime was ablaze with azaleas. I approached a realtor who introduced me to his wife, Mary. She had been a full-time mom, a part-time university administrator, and had recently received her realtor's license.

Mary took me to a dreary place she described as charming. Upon arrival, she said, "This will be perfect for you." I stiffened. She had no sense of how I related to space and was trying to define my emotions before they had even formed! This house made me queasy. It might have been the box-like rooms or Mary's preemptive attempts to structure my affect. Entering another house, she said, "You will love this one!" Knowing her approach would not work for me, I said, "You are very gracious, Mary, and I know you mean well. But I need to experience a house for myself. How about you silently watch and listen as I describe my feelings as we go from room to room. Then we will together discover how spaces impact me." She responded, "I've never done it this way before, but let's give it a try."

Meandering through the next house, I freely emoted. Some spots felt nourishing, others stirred my out-of-sort-ness. Mary was quietly attentive. As we left, she said, "I liked our experiment, but I know we do not have any place that's right for you. I'll look around and call once I find something promising."

A week later, Mary took me to a house that she knew was too expensive. She wanted to confirm that she had read me correctly. My instant reaction was "Mary, I love it. Find a place like this that I can afford, and I'll buy it!" Within days, she had located a home that was perfect. It was another realtor's listing, but that did not seem problematic! I signed a contract and gave Mary a deposit, which she handed to the primary agent who promised to call as soon as the deal was done.

The next day a very distressed Mary was on the phone. "There has been foul play. Soon after we submitted your contract, the listing agent found another buyer who offered less money. She set it up so the other party would win. Had you bought it, she and I would have split the realtor's fee. This way she gets the whole commission! I hate this part of our business. What upsets me most, though, is she put a rumor into the community that you are a financially shaky foreigner! My husband says you should sue her. But for now, there is nothing we can do."

Mary was so upset we agreed to talk in a few days, but first I told her that, as an untenured faculty member with a visa that had to be renewed each year, I knew it was easy to cast me as an economic risk! When we next spoke, Mary was still apoplectic. "I hate these back-stabbing games! This is the first time it has happened to me. I want to quit this job! Please find yourself another agent. I'm sorry that I failed you!"

My reaction was "I'd like to postpone our search for a while because I am really busy. However, you did nothing wrong, Mary. You can sack me as a client. But you are my realtor! That won't change." She thanked me and said she would be in touch.

Two months passed. Then Mary called unexpectedly, saying "The first house we saw that you really liked has not sold. The price has been reduced. If you are interested, I'd like it to be yours. It is still more than you can pay. I have decided to forgo my commission. That puts it in your price range. Your support during our fiasco helped me get back on my feet. I've had many weeks of great sales and having you in a home that's right for you would make me very happy!"

I was overwhelmed. Words usually come easily to me, but not on this occasion. As I held back my tearful appreciation, all I could say was "Thank you, Mary. I'll call you tomorrow!"

I got the Australian bank holding all my assets to wire them right away. Fortunately, the currency exchange rates were really favorable, so I called Mary to confirm that with the gift of her commission, I was able to buy this house. She was delighted.

Within weeks, I moved in. I loved living there. It was a home filled with emotional healing, rich memories of dinner parties, vigorous dancing, and joy-filled activities. It was a place that daily nourished me as I built a life for myself in this new land. During that period, I met Sara. We got married two years after I had relocated to Philadelphia.

REFLECTIONS ON BUYING A HOUSE

This seems to be just another generosity story. However, it was also about gratitude breeding generosity that spawned more gratitude, activating an abundance-multiplier effect.

This began with a simple process: listening. During our first outing, Mary tried to slot my emotions into a groove, so she could affect a swift transaction. She was dealing with something concrete, a house. However, I was searching for something illusive, a palliative for my restlessness. I asked Mary to connect with my emotions and to use the listening skills she had developed during her mothering years. Mary was yet to find her sea legs in the real-estate business. Her previous occupations had come to an end. Seeking a fresh start in her early 60s, she had joined this profession. However, everything in her life to date had made her a great listener. So, when I asked her to silently absorb my emotional responses to physical space, she went along with my proposal. Mary had correctly sensed my desires. I was grateful for how she had adroitly turned my amorphous feelings about physical spaces into something that could be operationalized.

After finding an ideal house for me that fell through due to a familiar cutthroat business practice, Mary was shell-shocked. She presumed I would want nothing further to do with her. That was not correct. I told Mary how grateful I was for all she was doing for me. She said, "No, you are the one who is being generous." While my support might have helped Mary a little, my role in her getting back on her feet was minimal. Mary did not see it that way. She had enjoyed weeks of excellent sales and felt grateful for everything in her life. Put simply, she wanted me to have this home, and she was willing to forsake her realtor's fee to make it happen.

That is when things got tricky, not publicly, but in my mind. I felt uneasy about accepting her offer. This level of generosity was too magnanimous. I was very touched by her gift, along with the affection it conveyed. However, I did not want to everlastingly feel indebted to her. I thought it would be awful if that inner disquiet of mine ended up tarnishing my experiences of being at home. Then it became crystal clear. Mary was not doing this for any reason other than it bubbled out of her very being. She was grateful for things I could not even comprehend but which needed a clear outlet. I had been partially instrumental in this, not because of what I did but by how Mary had constructed for herself the meaning of our interactions with one another.

Generosity arising from that level of gratitude, if it failed to find an appropriate recipient, was going to be like a stillborn child. Mary did not have any expectations of me. All she wanted was that I accept her gift. That is when I realized it would be stingy of me to reject her generosity or to water it down. It had to be all or nothing. Mary had taken a mere transactional exchange and made it relational. I had to decide if I would concur. That meant finding in me sufficient generosity to accept her gift. For Mary, this was not a monetary gift, but a gift of her very self. When I accepted, she oozed gratitude. The generosity of her gratitude made me grateful for her gratitude.

Mary died in her late 90s, a grandmother and great-grandmother of more than two dozen progeny and who knows how many adoptees like me! Across the decades, she has always been in my heart. And when I come home, albeit now in a different city, I am grateful to this lady for helping me discover the abundance associated with generosity begetting gratitude begetting generosity, each phenomenon midwifing the other.

GRATITUDE GALORE

Gratitude comes from the Latin term *gratus*, which means expressing effusive thankfulness. Uncontainable thankfulness catalyzes a circulation system that is self-sustaining, aiding and bonding both senders and recipients while also sprinkling the environs with restorative energies. Gratitude is a condition, an orientation. If it becomes an ever-present part of one's being, it may even grow into something called a personal trait akin to being highly attentive, outgoing, or considerate. However, gratitude can also be thought of as less solidified than a character trait, for it can be acquired by anyone who can then elect to turn it on or off like a faucet.

This image of a valve conjures a picture of pipes or arteries, which have narrow or wide apertures and can get clogged when filled with excess debris! Metaphorically, in many ways, gratitude and generosity have similar features to plumbing or a bloodstream. Generosity and gratitude both flow from one location to another. They are a force. They carry specific types of energy. They activate a reciprocating response. And they are channeled. Such an image resonates with us because we have all felt streams of gratitude and of generosity flowing into us and out of us with a measured or gushing force that inspires both sender and receiver.

Again, speaking metaphorically, drops of gratitude and generosity are like tears that can convey sadness or joy. Occasionally, each teardrop contains within it both deep sadness and intense joy. That is why in a single moment we can be weeping tears of exuberance and tears of anguish. Something similar occurs with generosity and gratitude. These two fluid forces can coexist, function fine separately, link up, or be decoupled when appropriate. As they flow in one direction, the drops transport generosity. When the path is reversed, they convey gratitude. At any moment, a globule can switch from being generosity to gratitude or vice versa. Droplets of gratitude or generosity are not one thing or the other but both, so when gratitude is sent, it can become experienced as generosity upon reaching the designated receiver. The converse is equally true.

A stream of gratitude can also be a stream of generosity. And a stream of generosity can be a stream of gratitude! That is indeed abundant! But notice again the presence of scarcity. There are limiting boundaries such as pipes, arteries, and levees that channel the flow in desired directions. These scarcity buffers prevent flows from being diffusely dispersed.

In earlier chapters we expounded on how trust, faith, and belief serve as significant abundance amplifiers. The same assertion can be made about generosity and gratitude. Not only do they contribute mightily to each other's growth, they magnify, intensify, and strengthen abundance. But let's remind ourselves once more that abundance is not about having excesses of everything imaginable but the right amounts of what is essential to fully be who we are.

Curiously, generosity, and gratitude are recognizable only when we are truly listening. This implies we are to tune into more than surface messages and attend to what may be hidden beneath, within, and beyond a sound, an utterance, a gesture. Multilevel listening is not easily mastered. It takes time, patience, and training to be competent at this form of hearing.

When seeking something, we tend to see only what we are looking for and fail to notice any thing other than what we desire. We can be so obsessed with a specific outcome we do not even register that other options of significant value are available. For a seeker to see alternatives, it helps to stop searching for what does not exist in that setting and to accept the prospect of embracing what is present. It is so easy for the very searching to be given such a high value that the only thing ever noted is the not finding.[2]

There is an irony associated with a biblical adage, *Seek and ye shall find!* Just as valid is its counterpoint: "Only when totally lost are we able to be found!" North American indigenous communities have a legend about feeling lost and being discovered. In nature we are never lost. If we don't know where we are, we can always stand still and listen. The trees, the birds, the squirrels are not lost. All the things around us know where we are. We are here with them. We are a part of nature. Nature knows where it is. We are here, with nature![3]

These thoughts about seeking apply equally to hearing. We are all selective listeners. If you do not recognize this, say to a teenager in a loud voice, "Please clean your bedroom." That bundle of adolescent energy is unlikely to hear that statement at all. But say quietly, "Who would like an ice cream," and the response will be a burst of exuberance. When predisposed to listen only to what we want to hear, we are unlikely to notice messages other than those we are expecting.

We can learn a lot by listening to nature in the same manner that nature listens. Nature has many voices. Consider a storm. It conveys many messages. It declares the arrival of new deposits of wetness. As thunderclaps reverberate around the landscapes, a storm's capacity to create chaos is announced. The thumping given to objects in its path are auditory signs of its direction and its force. Then, it the midst of an escalating cacophony, total silence and an eerie stillness appear, as if eternity has chosen to rest for a moment. This quietude announces that we are safe for a second or two, holed up in the center of something about to shatter the peace and splinter off in multiple directions. A storm's voices offer many bits of data.

Another way of saying the above is to draw an analogy with music. Depending on how we listen to music, we hear several voices. In Mozart's Requiem, for example, there are the voices of the orchestral instruments, of the lyrics telling a dramatic story, of the tenor, contralto vocalists, etc., and the many musical threads being interwoven into a majestic commemoration. As already discussed, humans hear sounds in a tiny range, although creatures around us have the capacity to hear well below and well above our level. Hence, when listening to nature's music, we miss a great deal and are unaware of what we are missing. Previously, we looked at sight and asked what we might see if we had a third eye or a fourth eye. What might we hear if we had many ears, instead of just two?

When striving to hear inner voices, which of course do not make any sounds, it often helps to say them aloud, so we can hear them! But what if I say things to myself but do not attend to what I said and hence misrepresent myself to myself? Listening to the messages coming from within is of great value. For some folk, praying serves this function. Others need a different modality to hear their deepest longings.

There is an old *Hindu* practice that illustrates this well. A person desiring to access unspoken inner messages can approach a stranger and ask that individual to be god for a few minutes. While there is no imperative to accept this request, it is an honor to be asked, so people usually agree.

During the event, the stranger listens with an embracing heart, as the speaker expresses what she or he needs to say aloud. Both people maintain an appropriate emotional distance. Once the person has finished giving voice to his or her pains, delights, thoughts, anguish, a period of silence follows. Then the god for the moment quietly leaves. And the originator of this overture lets the internal messages coming from her or his Higher Self sink into the soul's depths.[4]

Back to our core topic, and to summarize, despite the above complexities, we can discern the presence, tone, and magnitude of generosity and gratitude with the basic sensory and intellectual equipment we have. In addition, it is easy to recognize that the self-generating generosity-gratitude cycle is a version of abundance as well as an abundance amplifier.

A MERGING OF ABUNDANCE WITH ANCIENT PHILOSOPHIES

Some spiritual traditions such as *Christianity* proclaim that it is more blessed to give than to receive! *Taoism* states it is more blessed to receive than to give. There is a simple way to merge these two contradictory adages: *it is blessed to both give and to receive!* What is most clear about this back-and-forth-ness is we cannot give what we have not already received, and we cannot know what it is we are about to receive until it has been gifted to us. Also, a gift only really becomes a gift when received. The receptivity of the receiver is a gift to the giver. In addition, nature generously gave us our capacities to be receptive to generosity. Giving and receiving is such a two-way flow that forcing a distinction between them is meaningless.

One of the most generous streams that humans can access was described by *Lau-Tzu*. This channel is open to all. However it only operates for those who are grateful for what they have and who are not caught in the trap of feeling entitled to things. Here is one of *Taoism*'s most special gifts.

Lau-Tzu began his poetic treatise by proclaiming that before any thing existed there must have been an energy system so incomprehensible and so vast it should never be named. This idea is also in *Judaic* thought, which saw the divine to be so beyond us that speaking of it would desecrate it. Hence, *Judaism* chose four consonants, YHWH to symbolize the transcendent. This set of letters cannot be pronounced. But more importantly, it is a verb, not a noun. The early view of the *Jewish God* was not a *being* at all. YHWH is an old form of the verb *to be*, which decreed that divinity is understood *to be* located in the *actual doing* not in the doer.[5]

In *Taoism*'s case, having declared it is not possible to reason about things that cannot be named, *Lau-Tzu* chose to call this unnamable the *Tao*.[6] As previously discussed, the *Old Master* suggested we think of *Tao* as something akin to the *Universal Mother*, the vast empty womb from which all things and all non-things come into being. Of course, it is not a womb. That is a metaphor. *Lau-Tzu* used a readily accessible image, the womb, to indicate what *Tao* might be like, while also sounding a strong caution not to treat the name as being that to which the word is attached. Setting this complexity aside, these two foundational assertions by *Lau-Tzu* leave us with two grand paradoxes: (1) the *Incomprehensible* is named; and (2) this *Universal Womb* gives birth to all existing things and everything that never was but has the potential to be.[7]

From the outset, *Taoism* provides humanity a comforting sequence of thoughts: (1) accept that nothing of real significance can be fully grasped and that all thoughts, all emotions, all intuitions, all bodily sensations are always possible in any given moment; (2) that gives us the freedom to treat these parts of us as purely provisional; (3) if there is nothing fixed about a physical reaction, thought, intuition, feeling, the very act of naming it, inaccurate and inadequate though our chosen words may be, gives a temporary shape to that experience; (4) those tentative characterizations of these inner happenings let us encode what is going on in that particular moment. At the same time, we are instructed to accept that these sketchy body-mind-heart-spirit rumblings are not permanent. Hence, we are free, even advised, to discard them immediately. Then, into the void created by what we just let go of will rush other bodily sensations, thoughts, feelings, and intuitions. This pattern endlessly repeats itself.

Thus dawns a fresh realization. We are always living within streams of energy with no beginning or end. That energy is freely given. It is generous in the extreme. And if we can appreciate and be grateful for it, that generosity-gratitude cycle can be our lifelong sustainer. What a renewing, revitalizing, redeeming thought! We were all mothered by, and are continuously a part of, the universal mothering located deep within us! That is one overwhelmingly powerful manifestation of the abundance phenomenon. Reaching that level of acceptance means learning how to cope with considerable anxiety, a topic to be addressed later. Courageously listening to the messages contained in our anxieties is a wide-open gateway to an abundance mindset.

MOVING THE FOCUS FROM THE INTER-PERSONAL TO THE INTRA-PSYCHIC

Thus far I have spelled out the gratitude-generosity dynamic in inter-personal settings. As is clear from the *Taoist* discussion above, it is equally applicable to what is constantly occurring inside every person. One challenge of modernity is how to juggle competing priorities, how to keep it all together, how to be integrated. We all spend the bulk of our days trying to keep our bodies, minds, hearts, and spirits synchronized. This is blatantly visible during the teen and eventide years. The adolescent body shoots up but the intellect lags behind, or the mind races ahead and emotions freeze. And in our later years, the body may decline but the mind remains sharp, or the opposite.

We constantly wrestle with this issue of balancing our physical being, our emotional life, our intellectual acumen, and our spiritual condition. It is so acute it often cannot be adequately managed during waking hours and hence erupts during sleep, in our dreams.

I will illustrate the complexity of this intra-psychic integration challenge and the angst it stirs within and around us with a dream I had repetitively from my early adult years well into my forties. I will end this chapter with this dream. It presages the way anxiety opens new pathways to grasping the essence of abundance.

To contextualize this dream, readers need to appreciate the traumatizing impact of the Cold War upon my generation. It began when the atomic bomb obliterated Hiroshima and Nagasaki during World War II and came to an end during the Soviet Union's final days. Worldwide, people were conditioned to heed sirens announcing a potential nuclear fallout. This was a heavy pall permeating all of humanity. It was regularly reinforced by movies, images of mushroom clouds, or the Chernobyl and Three Mile Island catastrophes. I had the following dream dozens of times spread across two decades. It was so familiar I gave it a name, *my nuclear holocaust* dream.

There was a nuclear explosion where I lived. Most people died, and survivors were severely debilitated. I was one of only 50 people who were not injured. Rescuers came from around the world to clean up the mess, to help the wounded, and to seal the contaminated land. The unscathed were arrested and charged as enemies of the people who *knew about the nuclear risks but did nothing to stop it*! All my relatives and loved ones had perished. I was crippled by grief!

The whole dream occurred in a courtroom. Lawyers told us to plead *not guilty* and make the prosecution prove its case. This would be impossible because all records were destroyed by the blasts and there were no impartial jurors. In my dream, I wrestled with what to do. Even though my share was a billionth of the collective culpability, I felt guilty because I knew what was going on but had not taken any action to curb it. Since it seemed that humanity would completely destroy itself, it felt shocking to be alive! I was the only person pleading guilty. It was my way to be accountable for my contributions to environmental degradation. Although having no control over what so-called civilizations had created, I was ready to accept the truths this court was trying to address.

My guilty plea made me a curiosity and a convenient scapegoat for scads of troublesome societal travesties. TV cameras from many nations broadcasted my pathos. On the witness stand I was asked only one question. Once answered, there would be nothing left to say. The query? "If you knew about these nuclear dangers, why didn't you do anything to stop it?"

Through tears expressing my helplessness, I blurted out, "I couldn't think of anything to do! I knew it was happening and would destroy us. But I did not know how to change it. I could not make a difference, but I can't convince myself it is not my responsibility!"

That was usually the point when I awoke in a cold sweat, my whole body shaking. I never waited around in my dream to hear my sentence. Jolted into wakefulness, I would summon the dawn and then anesthetize myself with the busyness of the day. However, every time I was at this Nuremburg-like trial, a little piece of my inner armor was chiseled away.

One night, as I came to the conclusion of yet another gut-wrenching version of my nuclear nightmare, I had the temerity to stay asleep long enough to learn my fate.

In wakefulness, I could not imagine an appropriate dispensation. Would I be put to death? That was the same as perishing in the nuclear blast. Would I be sent to jail? The hidden walls made from the building blocks of my ineptitude, my helplessness, and my shame had already incarcerated me! There was no penalty that could ever match the pain of losing all my loved ones.

My guilt was accepted, and I looked at the judge. At that moment he ceased to be a person and became a disembodied, deeply resonant voice. He stated for all to hear, "Guilty as charged!" Although this conclusion was predictable, many in the courtroom gasped, probably because they identified with my blameworthiness.

Then came the sentence. It was something I had never expected. "You are *forgiven!*"

I woke immediately. I felt wrapped in the arms of eternity. And I fell asleep again. That was the last time I was visited by my nuclear holocaust dream.

There are many ways to interpret any dream. One that is helpful is to treat every character as a facet of the self. Using this technique, I found that a surface-level interpretation was sufficient for me. In my dream, I was part of the masses that had bought into demeaning the bad guys and lauding the good guys! I was the scurrilous, the accused, the prosecutor, the one above-it-all, the innocent, the guilty, the defense attorney, the jury, the judge, the standby executioner, and the disembodied voice. During my years of this dream's existence, I thought I had anticipated every possible outcome. I was wrong. Never once did I consider forgiveness.

Before this culminating moment, I had not appreciated how hard it is to forgive myself. It is much easier to forgive someone else or to have someone else forgive me. It is difficult to accept every element of the self and so we ask for others' acceptance. But even if the receiver of my displaced emotions were willing to be forgiving, I still have to live with myself 24 hours a day. And if I have not forgiven myself, another's forgiveness is but a window dressing briefly concealing the ways I hide from my deeper realities.

I experienced the endpoint of my dream as the most special grace moment of my inner life. The magnitude of that generosity left me with a big reservoir of gratitude that has never lessened. That was **THE** time that I was the most generous to myself, and I felt held and loved by some form of incomprehensible transcendence. It had taken years for that generosity to grow large enough to clear out decades of emotional and spiritual dross so I could receive my sentence. The gratitude for the self-generosity contained in that three-word sentence, *"You are forgiven,"* was redemptive.

SUMMARY

This chapter explicated the following themes:

- Generosity begets gratitude and gratitude begets generosity.
- Gratitude and generosity make each other possible.
- Failure can be both paralyzing and catalytic.
- Gratitude is a force, a flow of restorative energies.
- Generosity and gratitude are both gifts of nature.
- Abundance grows when gratitude-generosity flows freely.
- It is more blessed to be both giving **and** receiving.
- Only when a gift is received does it become a gift.
- Acceptance of a gift is a gift to the giver.
- The generosity-gratitude nexus amplifies abundance.

CHAPTER 7

NATURE'S EXTRAVAGANCES

Flowing from our past discussions, we could easily start addressing the themes of how abundance fosters a sense of belonging, how it guides our search to be at home in this world, and how it helps us accept the people we have become or are becoming. However, we will first take a detour into nature, the cosmos, and consciousness. When we return to the above, we will address the topics of anxiety, conflict, and belonging as they relate to the psychosocial sense of abundance.

As stated several times, nature is the greatest exemplar of abundance. We are fully aware of this when we plant a peach seed and watch it grow. In time, that tree will annually produce many luscious peaches, each of which is delightedly devoured by a range of creatures. And inside each peach is another seed that can be planted and will create a tree yielding more peaches, ad infinitum.

Our starting point has to be how we think about nature. There are so many marvelous ways to reason. Yet humanity's thinking capacities are handicapped when we reflect on *how we reason*. Symbols, languages, mathematics, analytics, etc., were invented by people, as were writing, storytelling, oration, music, and the arts.

When studying our thinking, the limitations of our thinking make it hard for us to grasp the restrictive character of our cognitions. This quandary called self-reference is like using a candle to investigate the shadows its flickering flame creates. Shining light upon darkness dissolves or distorts what we hope to find and informs us only about light's illuminating qualities!

Another dilemma is that all communication is murky. Utterances come from unique places. Listeners are tied to their own spaces. Words have meaning only if what they are affixed to can be recognized. A symbol is not *the* reality. It is only a hazy image of an object or happening. Accordingly, speakers and listeners have to infer what is beneath, within, or behind symbols that both signify and cloak what speakers and listeners are trying to make known.

Science calls for precision. Mathematics demands internal consistency and logical integrity. Philosophy tolerates fuzziness. Literature, poetry, and art are given license to play with concepts that collide, to dance around the self-contradictory, to make thinly veiled illusions that prop up or expose other hidden things. Consequently, several difficulties appear when different disciplines encounter each other, when East meets West, when antiquity tangos with modernity, when science duels with nature, when established patterns fuse with newly forming ones.

This chapter begins with a story about trying to convert an intelligence test designed for Caucasians into one that would be relevant for indigenous children, using their ancient logics rather than those made by modernity. That effort revealed substantial insights about how people living close to the earth both see and understand nature. Second, we will plumb what scientists say about nature, skirting across a broad landscape that attends to things like atoms, electrons, quarks, mini-solar systems, forces that bind and repel, antiparticles, the origins of the cosmos, fission, fusion, electromagnetism, gravity, galaxies, and the macrocosm-microcosm parallelisms. This was all addressed wonderfully by Neil deGrasse Tyson in his series on the *Cosmos*.[1]

We will then examine the parallelism between what modern science says about nature and what the ancient *Hindu* studies on consciousness revealed, as recorded in that famous poem, the *Mahabharata*. The alignment is breathtaking and haunting. We will keep punctuating this exploration with reminders that nature is the source of the abundance we rely upon and celebrate.

AN INDIGENOUS WORLDVIEW[2]

Australia's First Peoples have forms of awareness unfamiliar to urbanized modernity. An early adult experience led me to appreciate this. A graduate-student group I belonged to was trying to discover how indigenous children learn. We began by building an intelligence indicator in tune with their cultures, starting with measuring tools similar to those used in classic IQ tests. Today I cringe when thinking about this. Many of our views were off base and our group did not have any member of the community we were studying. This was understandable but inexcusable. Alas, the first indigenous Aussie to get a bachelor's degree received it in 1965. And a decade passed before one of those initial graduates was awarded a PhD.

We wanted to avoid linguistic problems when using our instruments, so all communication was done via mime. This worked well and created an active, playful discovery environment.

One element of intelligence tests is *memory span*, which is classically assessed by asking a child to repeat a sequence like 4-1-3-2. The number of digits is incrementally increased until the child can no longer accurately recall them. The average scores of all children for each age group are made into a base metric. Each child's performance can then be compared with that benchmark.

107

To create an equivalent gauge, we attached four blocks to a piece of wood.[3] The tester, who was a fellow grad student, or I took a block similar to those affixed to the frame and tapped out a pattern like 4-1-2-3-1-4-3, with the location of the block on the frame being privately designated a number. The child was given a block and gestured to mimic what the tester had displayed. Youngsters easily tuned into this procedure, providing what we imagined would be a good measure of memory span.

We quickly stumbled upon a startling finding. These children did not even look at the blocks as the tester tapped out a sequence, yet they could accurately repeat the order. Overall, they had outstanding recall. How did they do this? Clearly, they were using processes we did not recognize! This took a while to discover.

These children reproduced the pattern by reading the testers' eye movements. We researchers were not aware of the clues we were giving off as we scanned the blocks to record their responses. We had previously memorized the patterns and our eye movements were subtly signaling which block to tap next. To interrupt this practice, we began wearing caps that hid our eyes. Then these youngsters, who had been very engaged, lost all interest in this activity. They were engrossed when mapping our eye movements, but not when foolishly banging blocks together.

This opened up new streams of research as we began entering a world unknown to us. Australia's First Peoples do not store in their individual memory banks information that is accessible via other means. They do not think of the mind as located in individual brains but view each person as a small part of the collective mind. Accordingly, they chose not to fill everyone's brains with the same data. Instead, they developed sensing and thinking systems that were bridges to what we might today call a cyber-cloud. These students saw that the tester's intellect was available to them, so it made no sense to overload their own minds with facts that could be accessed in less burdensome ways.

While doing this research on indigenous intelligence, I spent a day on a deserted island with a group of these preteen lads. Climbing into a beat-up dinghy, I asked the organizer why we had not brought any food or water. He suggested I just watch how the day unfolded. Upon arrival after a three-mile ride, one boy shinnied 20 feet up a coconut tree. Soon it was raining coconuts. A whack on a pointy rock punctured the hard skin and soon everyone was heartily drinking nature's milk. At first sign of hunger, the boys took off in pursuit of a boar lurking in the thickets. It took an hour to catch that wild pig, which they slaughtered with a sharp rock. They dug a pit, filled it with logs, started a fire, and by early afternoon were feasting on roast pork.

They left half the carcass for other animals to eat. Sitting at a distance, these lads chuckled delightedly as birds, furry mammals, and lizards emerged from the bush to enjoy the banquet.

That day I was given quite a lesson on abundance. These boys believed that nature would provide whatever they needed. They were perpetually delighted by this adventure, and their gratitude was evident in how vigorously they approached each activity, especially finding a boar. They accepted that the pig might escape and if that happened, not having any food was fine. But if the boar was to be sacrificed, other creatures should also be fed.

These boys' thinking processes were quite easy to grasp. Some people consider knowledge to be a created commodity to be stored in libraries, computers, or cyberspace from which it can be retrieved. Others treat nature as a source of insights that ripen and fall like fresh fruit. Australian schools historically did not teach these ways of knowing, in part due to the educators' ignorance. And the indigenous elders were reluctant to share their secrets with others, justifiably fearing that their intellectual treasures would be desecrated and used to corrode their culture.

Experiences like these showed us how connected Australia's First Peoples are to nature: for them, earth is the eternal mother; the body is just a vessel temporarily housing their spirits;[4] and all meaning resides in the links between the earthly things and the spirit world. For these young people, tracing ghostlike footprints left by a kangaroo on the crust of sunburnt ground is noteworthy. A twig slightly dislodged, a smudge of dust redistributed since the last dew or a gentle indentation in the earth made by an animal in flight is significant. But silly numerical series are pointless!

Today, most of us value the Internet, a rather recent invention. However, the indigenous populations have benefited from nature's Internet for thousands of years. In 2016, Berman and Lanza, two well-respected scientists, wrote, "The mind is everywhere. It is everything you see, hear and sense...The brain is where the brain is and the tree is where the tree is. But the mind has no location."[5] For about 50 millennia[6] Australia's First Peoples had been operating in accord with this form of abundance, which has always been nature's modus operandi.

These First Peoples trusted what their senses told them, put their faith in nature, and believed in the trustworthiness of their environs. They embraced the streams of generosity surrounding them and reciprocated with comparable gratitude. They lived on the principle of enoughness and treated scarcity as a boundary system within which they were to function. They viewed limitations as an invitation to recalibrate. This mindset gave them a certainty that they belonged to one another, to the world around them, to the cosmos, and to the spirit world of which they were a part.

I have noticed similar patterns in the parts of India where there is little formal schooling. Educated helpers are surprised when tribal villagers ignore the agricultural proposals scientists develop. Graduate-educated specialists working in sustainable livelihoods arenas often feel their efforts will be of value only when these so-called illiterates learn to read. As an outsider, I have a different view. I see this as an encounter between people with two different forms of literacy. One has the literacy of literature, the other the literacy of nature. Professionals know how to read texts storing scientific findings. These villagers know how to read the sky, the winds, etc. Using tools passed on to them by ancestors who had studied geographical and meteorological patterns for centuries, they tune into nature's knowledge of itself.

By melding these two ways of knowing, another facet of abundance becomes clear. I will illustrate this in the coming pages by placing side by side the findings of modern scientific scholars and the studies of consciousness undertaken in India before the cognitive revolution, which occurred in several corners of the world about 2,500 years ago.

PLOWING HEADLONG INTO THE SCIENCES

The language of science is important. English used one word to represent *physics*. The Chinese called it *Wu-Li* (pronounced *Woo Lee*), which has many potential meanings. *Wu* can signify *matter* or *energy*, *mine* or *self*, *void* or *non-being*. *Li* means *universal order* and *organic patterns*. Hence, *Wu-Li* at one level can mean *arrangements of organic energy* or *beyond one's senses*.[7] At a higher level, it can imply *being enlightened about universal energy patterns*, or *phenomena that defy our sense-making apparatus*. Such conceptual flexibility indicates that knowing involves working with thought vessels equipped to hold divergent images. As notions like order-in-chaos, curvilinearity of time, black holes and fractals entered the vernacular, *Wu-Li* and *physics* began to look similar. However, most people still act as if the earth is flat, treat time as linear, and operate on principles the Greeks developed 2,500 years ago.

The word atom emerged from a fight between two early Greek scholars. One argued that pairs of complementary but opposite elements could preserve their essence when a merger with each other generated something new and different. The other guy asserted change is impossible, that all existence is invariable and unique. These adversaries[8] skirted around their conflict by labeling the stable condition as the *being* state and *becoming* the transitional process. They decreed that all substances are constant but can change when fractured or mixed with other ingredients. They also decided that everything material was constructed out of *basic building blocks* called *atoms*, defined as the *smallest indivisible unit of matter*.[9] Such thinkers, dubbed the *atomists*, treated matter as different from thought, spirit, motion, and energy. Their dogmas survived, and centuries later, even scholars like Newton were still clinging to a mechanistic view of a universe that was supposedly made up of indestructible, perpetually interacting atoms.[10]

When studies of subatomic particles showed that atoms had many components, physicists began describing atoms as being like mini-galaxies and a grain of sand as being full of empty space! Thereafter measurements were based on the manifestation of phenomena rather than on direct observations. In addition, the language used to represent data accessed by instruments became less precise.[11] This increased fuzziness troubled many who craved precision. Even greats like Bohr and Heisenberg were bereft when their experiments produced paradoxes that grew more intractable the harder they pushed for clarity. Ultimately, these men came to accept that the language of science was inadequate to describe nature.[12]

At the start of 21st century, this was how the once supposedly smallest particle called an atom was viewed. In the future, these images are sure to be revised, rediscovered, and reformulated.

- All objects, plants, creatures, planets, galaxies, etc., consist of the 80 stable atoms in the periodic table and some rapidly decaying ones, plus many rare earth elements.[13]
- Stable atoms appear to function like miniature solar systems, with electrons orbiting a cluster of protons and neutrons labeled the atomic nucleus.[14]
- Opposites attract. Due to positively charged protons, the negative charged electrons are bonded to an atom's nucleus.[15]
- Since they have the same charge, protons in a nucleus would fling apart, were it not for a countervailing, so-called *strong nuclear force* binding an atom's protons and neutrons.[16]
- The sun generates endless supplies of hydrogen, carbon, nitrogen, oxygen, the materials that constitute 96 percent of a human's body mass.[17]
- Attraction among neutrons offsets the protons' electrical impulse, stabilizing the nucleus. As proton to neutron ratios increase, the nucleus becomes unstable and starts to disintegrate.[18]
- Everything is made of atoms and sub-particles that are

perpetually moving, attracting one another when a small distance apart and repelling each other upon getting too close.[19]

- Electrons, towed or thrust toward protons housed in other atoms, can couple and produce molecules. Bonds that do not degrade partners' nuclei are called chemical reactions.[20]
- It is not yet known if electrons are divisible, but protons and neutrons consist of smaller sub-particles called *quarks* and a plethora of other unstable entities that decay rapidly.[21]
- Two of these sub-particles, *W-bosons* and *Z-bosons*, contribute to radioactivity and paired with the *photon*, a particle from which light is made, transmit the electromagnetic force.[22]
- Other bosons, called *gluons*, bind *quarks* together and make larger particles, while *Higgs-bosons* give some particles their mass.[23]
- Every particle has an *antiparticle*. When such opposites collide in a mutually annihilating event, a big burst of pure energy is released.[24]

For lay consumers of scientific knowledge, this is fascinating and humbling. We know so much and so little! And what will the thinking be in a few generations? Already as sub-particles are slammed into each other close to the speed of light it seems these miniscule bits might be tiny vibrating strings behaving like rubber bands boogieing in more dimensions than the standard four of spacetime.[25] However, it might be that the basic block is *a spin network of quantized loops of excited gravitational fields,* whatever that means![26]

There are, however, several foundational ideas no longer

questioned: every atom is 99 percent empty space; the relations among its component parts are defined by energy pulls and pushes tying them together or driving them apart; both opposing and complementary forces exist within the internal life of all things, in the surroundings within which an entity is embedded and in the relations among the internal and the external; the temporarily labeled *strong* and *weak forces* that bind some and unfasten other particles can act quite counter intuitively.

That is the micro-picture at the atomic level. What does this look like at the macro level?

PHYSICISTS ARE HISTORIANS

While physicists' theories and research methods are intriguing, after analyzing their data using the best mathematics available, interpreting their findings and announcing their conclusions, most of what they write is history. It is a history of the material universe, of applied mathematics, of human thinking about the world's origins. Although often ignored, time is always a variable in research, because every observation is an aftereffect. It takes a few nanoseconds for a retina to register an event 100 meters away. Traveling at the speed of light, sunrays reach earthlings eight minutes after being emitted. Evidence of an event on the edge of the Milky Way takes 100,000 years to reach us, 2 million if it comes from the next galaxy over. Stars faintly visible to the Hubble telescope may have died before creatures with eyes had even evolved.[27]

Based on their discoveries, physicists are rightly modest about making predictions. Here is a classic example of their dilemmas. They can describe the many behaviors of electrons orbiting a nucleus but not know where a particular electron is as it cycles around an atom's core. They are also troubled that observing alters the behaviors of objects they are investigating. Particles can appear as substances or vibrations depending on the character of the watching system. Plus, at times they have to disturb, or even create, what they want to observe, in order to get the data.[28] These thoughts about physics-as-history apply to every scholastic endeavor. That should be celebrated, not criticized.

The following represent what 20th-century physicists came to know about the cosmos, while also suggesting that there are still vast unknown frontiers beckoning the next generations of adventurous scientists:

- The universe/multiverse originated 13.8 billion years ago and continued to expand but at a variable pace.[29]
- Everything, from particles to galaxies, came from the clumping together of a few small basic elements created during or right after an inaugurating cataclysm labeled the big bang.[30]
- The sun, with a diameter 100 times the size of the earth,[31] has 99 percent of our solar system's mass but occupies only a trillionth of its space.[32]
- The nearest galaxies and our Milky Way are similar. Those farthest away seem a bit different and less developed. Beyond the universe's unidentifiable boundaries is endless darkness.[33]
- The darkness that was all pervasive before the big bang now surrounds everything and is full of transparent hydrogen and helium but seems not to have any manifest material coagulation.[34]

- Initially, hydrogen was so hot that fusion occurred, turning much of it into helium. As the cosmos cooled, everywhere was hydrogen and helium, plus a big background of microwave radiation.[35]
- Flowing from the great beyond is a form of unrecognizable, unknowable energy.[36]
- As stars burn out, their helium becomes the materials from which the whole world is made, giving literal validity to the metaphoric adage *we are in the universe and the universe is in us.*[37]
- Gravity's impact and system instability increase in tandem. The more the universe diverges from uniformity, the greater gravity's influence on the combining of basic elements.[38]

This tiny piece of physicists' grasp of the universe is very complex but is probably only a smidgen of what will be known someday. Setting that aside, scientists declare that the three major and one smaller governing principles of our material universe are fission, fusion, electromagnetism, and gravity, respectively. But to explain their findings, these pillars have required the addition of what was once called a *hypothetical mathematical variable.* They now think that this *hypothetical* is *real* but *unknown.* It is referred to as *dark matter* and *dark energy.* Combining all the known components of the cosmos, together they constitute only 4 to 5 percent of the universe's mass and energy! The other 95 percent they call *dark matter* and *dark energy.*[39]

What is *dark matter,* and what is *dark energy?* The distinction is twofold: dark energy repels and affects the entire universe; dark matter attracts and impacts individual galaxies. Stated differently, *dark matter*'s pulling together operates at the micro level, and *dark energy's* pushing away is at the macro level.[40] This *dark anything* must be a misnomer! It is *invisible, transparent,* and can *pass through objects,* leaving no identifiable trace of its presence or its pathways. Both *dark matter* and *dark energy* are tags linked to such incomprehensible phenomena that they are mostly terms cataloging our ignorance.[41] Some aspects of these forces have been estimated but knowledge about them is scant.[42] Ultimately, understanding these ideas would be simpler if they were relabeled *invisible energy systems* or *yet-to-be-understood energies,* which *attract* or *repel.*

Here is a summary of the scientific view of reality at the start of the third millennium CE. The Milky Way is one of hundreds of billion galaxies. Each galaxy has billions of stars, planets and moons, clouds of gas, dust, cosmic garbage, etc., that produce all the mass and energy, which is packaged in many forms. There are other energies from radio waves to X-rays that travel at the speed of light. However, every thing and every known form of energy in this universe extends almost 14 billion light years in all directions, irrespective of which planet is used as the center-point. And it accounts for less than 5 percent of the mass and energy![43] These *unknown or invisible energies* endlessly impact everything going on within and around the materialized five percent. But we cannot see, measure, or have any awareness of it!

In 2009, I had a chance encounter with one of the top astrophysicists of the 20th century, a man who had been a long-standing colleague of Carl Sagan. I asked him to give me a summary of the essential scientific findings during his career. He reaffirmed all of the above. And then I posed to him five questions, which for decades had been hanging out in the back of my mind. This is a slightly abbreviated version of what he said.[44]

Question 1: As the big bang birthed a universe built on electromagnetism, fission, fusion, and gravity, which for brevity's sake I will call *our universe*, might one or more other universes built on totally different principles have also come to life at the same time?

Response: **It would be a logical absurdity to assume otherwise!** However, because we exist in *our universe*, we could never know what any alternate universe is like!

Question 2: Could there have been big bangs before the one that happened 14 billion years ago?

Response: **It would be a logical absurdity to assume otherwise!**

Question 3: Is it possible that the big bang of 14 billion years ago also generated *alternate universes* that operate on principles other than fission, gravity, etc.?

Response: **It would be a logical absurdity to assume otherwise!**

Question 4: Might the 95 percent of *invisible energies* (*dark matter* and *dark energy*) of our universe result from interactions with other universes that are based on different principles?

Response: **It would be a logical absurdity to assume otherwise!**

Question 5: Humans talk a lot about consciousness, which is hard for us to grasp. Might the consciousness in our universe be influenced by the consciousnesses of alternate universes?

Response: **It would be a logical absurdity to assume otherwise!** But humans will only ever know the portion of that mega-consciousness this fits with our consciousness!

Of course, I have no idea if my questions where the right ones or if this expert's answers were correct, but this chat increased greatly my appreciation for the beauty of the mysterium.

THE CONSCIOUSNESS-SCIENCE NEXUS

There is a long tradition in India of studying the nature of consciousness using meditative techniques. This was at the core of *Hindu* and *Buddhist* practices. However, some of the most lucid writing on this topic is the *Mahabharata*, home of the *Bhagavad Gita*.

While *Taoists* avoided naming or making a deity out of the universals, which they think of as *Ultimate Reality*, *Hindu* writers did the opposite. They assigned descriptors to the *unnamable* and proposed a plethora of divine images that people could choose to worship.

Those unfamiliar with *Hindu* traditions may wonder why there are so many gods and why people want a personal god. Gandhi had a straightforward response. Our personhood is the only way humans can relate to anything. He also advised us to not think of god as having human attributes, only to recognize that this is all humans are able to grasp.[45]

The attributes of the divine are boldly displayed in the *Mahabharata*, a segment of which is titled the *Thousand Names of Vishnu*, the *preserver and sustainer of life* who is *concurrently* everywhere. This masterpiece treated *Vishnu* as synonymous with *Krishna* and *Rama*. Hence, they are viewed as interchangeable.

Original Chinese representations of the *Ultimate Reality*, the *ground of being*, the *oneness of all things* were abstract and metaphoric. Indians tended to concretize them. *Taoism* used noun images that encourage the cherishing of amorphousness and uncertainty! In contrast, *Hindus* assigned *divine qualities* to *Ultimate Reality*, giving each specific names and making strip-away-all-ambiguity assertions about their actions, such as *Vishnu, gives...Krishna is...Rama inspires...*! The Indian tendency is to plant the *incomprehensible* within the familiar. However, this does not imply that a *Hindu god's character* could ever be defined.

As previously stated, in the introduction to this book, this material on *Taoism* and *Hinduism* is best absorbed when we put aside our intellectual misgivings about peoples' deity-affirming, deity-creating, or deity-assigning impulses. For this moment, please focus solely on the cosmological word pictures conveyed within the *Mahabharata*.

Long before the scientific era, using meditative and deeply introspective approaches to ones' inner realities along with what was observable in nature and the night skies, Indians were able to sense, intuit, and develop images that in hindsight parallel a remarkable number of scientific views.

I have rephrased and clustered under seven categories the *Hindu* portrait of the cosmos and existence, nestled in the *Mahabharata*'s *Thousand Names of Vishnu*.[46] My goal in doing this is to exhibit the similarities between these ancient observations and contemporary science. I hope to show how the *Hindu* practice of placing people's inner landscapes under the microscope produces word pictures similar to the visual ones produced by modern telescopes probing the night skies. To remove deity language from this task, I use *Ultimate Reality* in place of *Vishnu*.

1. Ultimate Reality made all things. And all that exists is a mini-embodiment of Ultimate Reality.

Ultimate Reality, life itself, is the universe,[47]
> The womb of the cosmos,[48]
> The seed of all,[49]
> The totality from which all creation flows,[50]
> The self-existent,[51]
> The eternal spirit.[52]

Ultimate Reality, self-created at the beginning of time, is the foundation of the world,[53]
> The infinite whose forms are countless,[54]
> The unborn giver of life,[55]
> The earth, the sky, the heavens,[56]
> The fire,[57]
> The water lily, the jasmine, the oleander.[58]

2. Ultimate Reality is the energy in and the energizer of all creation, the sustainer, and the sustenance.

Ultimate Reality, ordainer, bestower[59] and refuge, travels to all places, [60]
> Knows everything,[61]
> Keeps time turning,[62]
> Makes reality increase,[63]
> Gives vitality,[64]
> Shines forth.[65]

Ultimate Reality, the vital energy,[66] the resting place of all supports[67]

    Fixed the sun with a thousand rays,[68]
    Conquered itself yet is never owned,[69]
    Sustained the worlds through countless eons,[70]
    Defined itself without definition,[71]
    Reduces all to its essence.[72]

3. Ultimate Reality is the essence in and of all things.

Ultimate Reality, the Being, the Self in every creature,[73] is the knowing of the senses,[74]

    The light of the sun,[75]
    The rays of the moon,[76]
    The cosmic sound,[77]
    The sweet season of the spring,[78]
    The twinkling of the eye.[79]

Ultimate Reality, the wise, courageous, dangerous, grateful, self-possessed, gracious[80] is

    Ever-patient,[81]
    Benevolent,[82]
    The dwelling place of goodness,[83]
    The healer,[84]
    A deep pool.[85]

4. Ultimate Reality is hidden, immeasurable, and unknowable.

Ultimate Reality, eternally fixed,[86] formless,[87] but with many hidden forms,[88]
> Is the measure[89] but
> Cannot be measured,[90]
> Cannot be described,[91]
> Cannot be understood,[92]
> Cannot be reached with words.[93]

5. Ultimate Reality is the one and the many,[94] the eternal now, as small as the tiniest object and as large as the universe.[95]

Ultimate Reality that extends in all directions,[96] is the child of the infinite,[97]
> The eternal and most ancient,[98]
> The past, present, future,[99]
> The one beyond birth, old age and death,[100]
> The unborn ruling all,[101]
> The cycles of the seasons.[102]

6. Ultimate Reality is the attractor and the attracted, the repulsion and the repelled.

Ultimate Reality is the one bringing all together[103]
> The majesty of the thunderbolt,[104]
> The purifier, the highest blessing,[105]
> The determination, the perseverance,[106]
> The abyss[107] and the bridge between the worlds,[108]
> The union of day and night.[109]

7. *Ultimate Reality is the change, the changer, the permanence, the stabilizer, the transformation, and the transformer.*

Ultimate Reality, which creates and destroys,[110] changes and changes not,[111] is
> The firm foundation of all things,[112]
> The unborn[113] and the deathless,[114]
> The unmoving[115] and the constant,[116]
> The done and the left undone,[117]
> The perishing and the imperishable.[118]

Please note how the above word pictures reflect the below scientific images discussed earlier in this chapter.

Everything existing at a microscopic or a macroscopic level
is made of the same elements.
Activities of and in the miniscule and the behaviors
of the gigantic mirror each other.
Everything that appears real and substantial is mostly empty space.
What is currently knowable is infinitesimally small.
Past, present, and future are one and the same.

The infinite, universal, and endless are present in the finite,
in the particular, in the time-bound.
Invisible forces are constantly impacting the character
and actions of everything.
All things benefit and suffer from being drawn together
and being pushed apart.
The most impactful energies cannot be identified or measured.
What previously happened there is now happening here.

SUMMARY

The major lessons unpacked during this chapter are:

- The sun has 99 percent of our solar system's mass but occupies only a trillionth of its space.
- Each atom is 99 percent empty space, so every object we see is 99 percent emptiness.
- This emptiness is the incubator of possibilities.
- Microscopic and macroscopic things have the same elements.
- Ultimate Reality is in the tiniest particles and in the largess of the cosmos.
- Collective actions of electrons can be predicted but not the conduct of a specific electron.
- Atomic particles' actions depend on how they are observed.
- The abundance that is in the outer world is equally present in our inner world.
- Ninety-five percent of the energy in the cosmos is invisible, transparent, and unknown.
- Abundance is Ultimate Reality, hidden, and immeasurable.

CHAPTER 8

LONGING TO BELONG

This chapter enters the third domain of abundance. The first layer was the *yin-yang* dynamic, which carefully calibrates just-enoughness. Streams of generosity and of gratitude, which constituted the second level, feed the psychological sense of abundance that sustains individuals, groups, organizations, communities, and societies. The third dimension of abundance consists of many well-known human processes. I will discuss just three: belonging, conflict, and anxiety. As with trust, faith, belief, generosity, and gratitude, this domain is also enveloped by and contributes to that great but incomprehensible phenomenon, consciousness.

We begin with another indigenous story. Boca, a young man, was about to be court-martialed for "going walkabout without prior approval." This event turned into a reenactment of Australia's long-simmering racism, as Boca tried to honor his tribal traditions and to gain acceptance within an all-white establishment. Soon he was being victimized for making visible the brutality of a military institution that had long shunned his peoples.

In this chapter, three third-layer abundance dynamics are introduced: belonging, conflict, and anxiety. The first being made central is belonging, with the other two serving as the backdrop. At the core of the fitting-in process is the conflict between the parts of us that want to be both *a part* of and *apart from* the groups, organizations, and institutions we populate. The struggle to belong, a source of suffering for many of us, is catalyzed by the angst that creates conflict and the conflicts that create anxiety.

During Boca's military tribunal, the officers recognized their need for a new form of consciousness. They wanted a fresh perspective on racial dynamics, indigenous legends, and the conflicts that frequently lead to scapegoating. While delving into the emotional morass that some antiquated military practices had manufactured, the relevant units came to see and understand each other's anxieties. Those shared anxieties led to a solution that brought to light a form of abundance previously unrecognized by the main actors in this drama.

In the ensuing pages, I draw upon three complex, but highly useful psychosocial aids: consciousness raising, legends, and some basic *Buddhist* teachings. The focus is on three themes: abundance is created when conflicting parties affirm their mutual anxieties and elect to build a common ground based on their shared distress; as with air and the Internet, an abundance of consciousness and consciousness of abundance is everywhere; abundance gets blocked when empty meanings are attached to things, thoughts, and emotions but is unleashed when people shed their attachments to worthless things.

REDIRECTING SCAPEGOATING ENERGIES

Boca, a valued member of the Australian Armed Services, suddenly disappeared, an offense that normally led to a court martial. To their great consternation, the military police could not find this man who returned after six days, acting as if he had never left. And the lawyers could not make any sense of Boca's story. He had been on a spiritual retreat with some fellow wayfarers. When asked where he had gone, Boca said "nowhere," describing his absence as lasting only a few minutes, not the six days recorded by a clock. His experience was similar to a daydreaming moment any worker might use to relieve a little bit of the day's drudgery. A senior military officer intervened and asked the psychological services unit I was employed by, to help Boca conform to military rules. Although the Defense Department cared for those damaged during combat, it had never developed policies to support indigenous personnel's ways of sustaining their mental health.

Several things are key to this indigenous practice: the sudden need for time away can arise spontaneously; resisting such an urge dishonors the moving of the spirit; the familiar forms of space and time get replaced by a spacelessness and timelessness similar to what happens in dreams; and one has to be willing to go *there*, albeit for a brief period, to continue staying *here*.

In our conversations with Boca, the secrets of his inner life were respected, and no psychological labels were attached to his actions. Led by a fiery Irish boss, psych services advised officialdom to treat this as two cultures colliding. We proposed that the military consider adjusting to Boca rather than demanding he adapt to them. Although this unauthorized leave had a different form and meaning than mental health or vacation days, the similarity was striking, since time in nature is usually curative and sanity preserving.

We asked the officer in charge what he would have done if Boca had a crisis at home and needed time to deal with it? His reply was "I would advise him to use some of his standard leave days." Psych services recommended that this officer adopt the same approach by keeping a stash of leave forms pre-signed by Boca. Then when Boca needed a spiritual break, his supervisor could submit the documents to cover his absence.

129

The senior officer accepted this proposal. It worked well for everyone. Boca continued to serve competently in this noncombat position and was in all other regards well suited to military life.

MUTUALLY BUILDING NEW INSIGHTS

This event had many features. First, this cacophony was inherently consciousness raising. The culture clash was clear. Everyone understood the conflicts. Although the fears aroused by this race and ethnicity-based conundrum could have caused anyone to press a scarcity button, no one did. All willingly looked at the scene with a fresh perspective and participated in cocreating a compatible solution, even though no single party would have chosen that particular path. This did not become a soul-crushing scapegoating of Boca. Throughout, no one sought an excess of anything, not compliance, nor self-authorized autonomy, nor power, nor recalcitrance, nor prestige. Everyone was content with having a mutual enoughness.

Second, this conflict was real and had serious consequences. It had begun when the UK made Australia into a penal colony. Many convicts, who in some cases had only stolen bread to feed their starving children, were shipped to the Antipodes for the rest of their days. Having criminalized poverty at home, the British deposited their domestic problems on the other side of the world, which resulted in a crime of much greater significance, the systematic obliteration of the indigenous people and their culture. For a long time, incarcerated and immigrant Australians tried to disregard this historical debacle. Without much consciousness, their conscience was protected from feeling culpable for their predecessors' actions. Such selective forgetting let each generation ignore these scandalous discriminatory practices. And without an active conscience about

Australia having been made a place solely for white people, new settlers from Europe were content to remain uninformed about the First Peoples' plight. Boca's case caused several high-ranking members of the Australian Armed Forces to scrutinize what our nation had been avoiding. The problem of this one individual was small, but this devastating discord symbolized what this new country had repetitively reinforced.

Third, Boca gained a level of acceptance, which made him feel special rather than shunned. The military learned about the cruelty of policies that crushed the spirits of those who were not part of a Eurocentric heritage. Security police discarded some pointless practices. Lawyers stretched the normal military boundaries and accepted the legitimacy of indigenous lore. Psych services and senior officers came to understand that the First Peoples had never laid claim to any land because for them the earth was the divine. So, when colonial powers seized the continent, its first inhabitants lost their way of life and access to the wide-open spaces, which were their spiritual sanctuaries.

Fourth, there were a number of people struggling with anxiety during those days. Boca was afraid that being dishonorably discharged would bring shame to his revered elders, who had been proud of his admission to such an esteemed institution. Boca's ejection for honoring his tribal practices would have cast a shadow on his people and kept inflaming their legitimate anger over this country's racism. The Department of Defense was disturbed about its role as a testing ground for a civil rights case, which it had not created but was obliged to address. Having failed to apprehend Boca, the police were worried about looking inept. The lawyers were fretting over how to integrate national law and the values of the First Peoples. Psych services were concerned that their proposal might make the military reactionary. Amazingly, no party pushed its anxieties aside but made those emotions into a common connector. That built a collaborative spirit and everyone was willing to implement a simple solution invented by an Irish immigrant.

Fifth, this event increased the sense of belonging among all who were involved. Boca was very tied to his own culture, which was such a large part of him he would not have been true to himself had he severed those bonds. He was also tethered to a system that treated his people as backward. Yet he liked the structure and predictability of service life because it counterbalanced the organicness of his former village existence. The officers boosted their own sense of belonging. Embracing a man slated for a dishonorable discharge opened them to a facet of their own honorability. The Defense establishment accepted that it had been the creator of Boca's bind. From then on, all these people belonged more fully to their own innate humanity and to each other.

There is another dynamic hidden inside the Boca story that is familiar to every one of us. It is managing how to simultaneously be *a part of* and *apart from* the dynamics of the human systems we live and work within.[1] The desire for inclusion activates fears of consumption, absorption, and deindividuation. The wish to be separate and independent generates fears about exclusion, aloneness, and isolation.[2] This ambivalence, which is natural, invariably gets muddied by, and contributes to, the murkiness of all institutions.

At the basic level, a group, an organization, a community does not want all of what its members are able to contribute. Groups and organizations choose to incorporate only the bits of each individual that are deemed as good for the collective, even though this may be harmful for the individuals. They then ask these same people who feel cherry-picked and truncated by that system to act as if those unwanted parts of their selves are irrelevant. Humans have to do something with these feelings, and we typically blame others or the larger system for our delegitimized emotions. Upon displacing such feelings onto others, our sense of belonging to ourselves and with those whom we are interdependent is lessened.

Like every person, Boca carried inside his identity, many groups, such as race, gender, class, age. But in this specific setting, it was his membership of two very different cultures that was most taxing. There were things about indigenous life he experienced as limiting. He was also aware of having talents and aspirations that would not be realized had he chosen to spend all his days in his place of origin. Yearning for something more than what he already had, Boca thought he could acquire this by befriending something foreign. He appreciated the comforts of familiarity, but that safety also dulled his curiosity, narrowed his field of vision, and sapped some of his energies.

He was attracted to the military because it was the antithesis of what he knew. He imagined the armed forces would force him to discover new things. However, he was afraid he would never fit into their structures. He was not white, he had never played the sports his peers were fanatical about, he did not know their music, and he could not get their vibe. In all areas, his learning curve was steep, and he was afraid he would always be an outsider.

Meanwhile, his feelings about his heritage were still strong, but there were few outlets on a military base to express them. For Boca, that pressure cooker was just as cramping and limiting as village life. As a misfit in both of these two worlds he sought the non-institutionalized environs of nature, the only place where he felt he fully belonged.

Many poets have written about our being born and dying in a state of wholeness, with the decades in between being fragmenting. Early childhood sustains an innocent wholeness, which starts to splinter as separateness, autonomy and agency develop. The things that shatter our youthful naiveté leave us with resultant vulnerabilities that both curate our maturation and punctuate our ripening with occasional regressive episodes.

We long for a sense of belonging and equivocate over whether to try gaining it by staying right where we are in our current forms and shapes. The alternative is to give our beings a makeover and to seek a fresh belonging in an unknown place that has yet to be found or created.

Typically, we seek to resolve these feelings by focusing on externals. Yet our real wish is to work out how to belong to the bodies, cognitions, emotions, and spirits we have. We often fret about how to get our physicality, our intellect, our feelings, and our spirits into a form that is likeable to both self and other. These two worlds, the one *that is* and the *one that might be*, become the fulcrum of our vacillations.

The reality is that in every setting we both belong and don't belong at the same time. We only know we are *here* because we know there is a *there*, which we discovered by learning about *here*. Do we belong here or there? Of course, upon arriving *there*, it becomes our new *here*, so it is never possible to belong anywhere but *here*, even though we may feel we do not belong *anywhere*. Belonging and not belonging, as with light and dark, are in the *yin* and *yang* of existence. When we fully belong to ourselves, it is possible to have a sense of belonging everywhere, even in places emphasizing our non-belonging.

THE TRUTHS ABOUT LEGENDS

I want to discuss two issues about the legends of Australia's First Peoples. But first it is important to acknowledge that all theories, all stories, all myths are created by biological systems that upon sensing the world, label what we see, smell, hear, taste, and touch. We then attach descriptors and meanings to these events. So-called *reality* is made by entities that have both a sensorium and a capacity to grasp the influence of that sensing system upon our experiences. Even things like spacetime and consciousness are products of mind and the languages used to represent them.

The material world, our sense of it and our thoughts about it, are substrata of each other and of consciousness. For example, when astrophysicists research spacetime, they are both studying and remaking consciousness as much as they are investigating something external that they presume would exist even if there were no supposedly conscious beings. People rarely reflect on time or space, which we treat as self-evident when walking a city block, running late for work, celebrating a birthday, anticipating winter, or erecting a barn. Life and our biological wiring lead us to think of spacetime as having an existence separate from experience. While it goes against the grain to imagine that creatures are the creators of time and space, we know these concepts are not objects that can be felt or smelled.

Spacetime, like gravity, is intangible. It is an interpretation of what is sensed. Physicists have known this since discovering that sub-atomic particles are both matter and energy. They can appear to be material objects when observed in a specific way but left unobserved or looked at through different lenses they are like waves or vibrations. Unlike the ones washing a shoreline, these are

135

probability waves in a statistical sense, which elucidate only free-flowing patterns and cannot be used to predict an action of any component part of a wave.[3] It is hard to picture how the cosmos and consciousness choreograph their dance, but physicists now operate as if a relationship does exist!

For ages, scientists treated the observer as a problem. However, the need for observers makes it impossible to disentangle the material world and consciousness. Again, we run into the Bertrand Russell problem. Materiality and consciousness are different logical types, are worlds apart that are entangled. However, it is difficult to build viable bridges between them.

Although scientists state that nothing travels faster than the speed of light, they know that distinct phenomenon can have seemingly instantaneous connectivity despite the huge distances separating them and not having any known means of communication.[4] With waves and force fields, a particle or cluster of particles can be anywhere. This implies entities and information might be floating in a paddock of resonance, in a form of mind-field unconstrained by classic spacetime laws. An example is a person who experiences an instantaneous knowing when a loved one is in medical trouble or dies, even if she or he is on opposite sides of the globe.

Historically, the average Aussie tended to disregard the legends of the First Peoples. To make black people as white as possible, Australian powers that be had in the past tried to undermine the legitimacy of indigenous myths. However, previous attempts to discredit their beliefs usually failed. For 50,000 years[5] these legends carried the people's communal knowledge.[6] Their ancient accounts were constantly fact-checked to preserve their authenticity as they were passed from generation to generation. If there was a slight deviation in any retelling, they were quickly corrected.[7] As it has turned out, many things the First Peoples thought were true, which the colonial authorities dismissed, were actually based on reality. Here are two stark examples.

First, the people in a remote region of central Australia's deserts had an ancient legend describing the decent of a fiery ball that had come down from the sun, killing almost everything. Scientific evidence indicates this was a meteor that crash-landed there about 4,700 years ago.[8] As it broke apart, the meteor would have been a huge blaze as large rocks with molten metal crashed into the earth, producing several craters.[9]

Second, the Gunditjmara people in the state of Victoria have a legend about a gigantic wave coming inland, killing everybody except those living on specifically named mountaintops. The legend about this ancient flood had been documented in pre-colonial times. Recently, geological samples of ocean sediments were found very close to the place referred to in the ancient indigenous accounts. These earth samples indicate there had been a tsunami that was a part of dramatic rising and falling of sea levels sometime between 9,000 and 5,000 BCE.[10]

It is valid to doubt a legend's veracity. However, its value is not tied to historical accuracy. Far more important are the truths we see in them that nurture, unsettle, or transform us.

THE DILEMMAS AND DELIGHTS OF CONSCIOUSNESS

What has been said about legends also applies to consciousness. We can debate if our take on consciousness is correct or we can be enchanted by its mysteriousness. However, we want to know about *this thing that is not a thing* called consciousness, of which we are a part. It is tough to belong to something we can't comprehend. Alas, those who try to study consciousness or the cosmos are required to be both fully inside and fully outside it at the same time, which of course is impossible. That form of straddling leaves investigators rudderless, because it is a struggle to fully belong to it without losing our connections with all the other important parts of ourselves.

This disturbance can be either a push or a pull. It might pull us in because being cradled by consciousness is comforting. Or it might push us away because we are treading water in an ocean of uncertainty. Both the pushes and the pulls can be happening at the same time. Those able to endure the conflicts, the dual tensions when exploring consciousness are teetering on the same *yin* and *yang* fulcrum that is at the heart of abundance. Here the *a part of* and *apart from* conundrum is alive and well. When we have cycled through this a large number of times, it is possible to discover that we need to be *a part of* to be *apart from* and we need to be *apart from* to be *a part of*. This creates a predictable loneliness and a craving to belong.

Ironically, aloneness begets belonging and belonging begets loneliness! When we realize this, the desire to be *a part of* and *apart from* feels very special. Who among us has the courage to stand on the boundaries between full immersion and total isolation, between attachment and detachment, between knowing nothing and knowing there is nothing to know! But those who are able to find a way of being fully in and fully out can discover … Here, the sentence must end, for we cannot know in advance what any individual will find!

We previously touched on ancient studies of consciousness and its parallelisms with science. Although we cannot state what consciousness is, it seems to reside within, beside, above, beneath, beyond the material world. But consciousness cannot be substantiated by science or philosophy. It does not appear to have a physical structure or to function like a library keeping records of how cells, elements and organisms act. Consciousness appears to be everywhere and nowhere in particular. We sense its stable and fluctuating presence but cannot say how it impacts us. We reach out to it and are touched by it, but we cannot touch it.

Grammatically, consciousness is a noun (*consciousness is all-pervasive*). It is a condition (*she is out of her coma and is conscious*). It is an adjective (*please attend our consciousness-raising session on gender*). It can be part of a verb (*please get conscious* of, i.e., figure out, determine). It is also used as a surrogate for mind, awareness, memory, cognition, awakening, mindfulness, implying these are similar phenomena, regrettably, because they are not the same!

Consciousness is both a phenomenon we try to grasp and a process of comprehending. What we strive to understand might be real, fiction, or illusion, but it seems to be some*thing*, even if it is only a figment of our individual or collective imaginations. When we reflect on this substance-less *thing* and the methods used to probe it, ambiguity dominates because the self-reflexivity of using consciousness to study consciousness is far more complex than normal thinking. That makes studying consciousness hard but special, not because we can master it, but because our attempts to do so open us to insights that cannot be accessed via reason.

We cannot make many meaningful statements about consciousness. Although a comforting concept, consciousness also gives us intellectual headaches. I will state a few of these brain-crunchers as questions to provide some parameters that can keep our considerations about consciousness contained. Having these unanswerable questions in mind keeps us humble and helps us to live in the mysterium rather than trying to remove mystery from our living! Here are a few boundary-setters.

Is consciousness the creative force making manifest the cosmos? Or reversing the causal streams, does the cosmos create consciousness? Are the cosmos and consciousness mutually cocreating? Or are they a unified phenomenon synchronously expressing the same thing? Or are they both products of another source? Is the manifest knowable only when both cosmos and consciousness are present? Or is knowledge about either possible only in the domains where these two phenomena are aligned, or solely in the dimensions that are alike? Can the processes of and the objects of consciousness be disentangled?

Most writers imply that everything we claim to know about the cosmos and the material world is limited to *human knowing*. *Consciousness* is a term people invented and attached to an indescribable, so this supposed knowing probably reveals more about human cognition than it does about what we claim to be discussing.[11] To avoid having to constantly repeat this, I am going to state my concern about discussing consciousness. When using this word, we put it in a sentence structure that makes it seem like we are reifying an idea and then acting as if that reification is reality.

I will be explicit and declarative: when using the word *consciousness*, I am talking about *a seemingly unknowable, amorphous phenomenon, which we sense is present and impacts everything. However, like YHWH and the Tao, this is a humanly created concept that names the inexplicable and then helps us discuss the incomprehensible.* It should never be presumed to be anything more than that![12] The same could be said about the *cosmos*. We know a lot about the vastness to which we belong, but we cannot state what makes existence or what lies beyond that which is! While stating anything definitive about consciousness is impossible, many have set off on this fool's errand. But doing so is no more of a folly than avoiding it.[13]

It appears that our formulations of consciousness are expanding, which is both beneficial and problematic. We want more knowledge about consciousness because it seems to be about to change.[14] Until recently, humanity was constrained by its biological limits, but no longer![15] Genetic engineering raises ethical concerns, for we can now modify genes faster than we can determine the implications of such advances.[16] We are already combining inorganic and organic components and human-IT interfaces are rapidly altering cognitive processes.[17] What will happen when individual brains and remote computers are connected?[18] We might like genome mapping and personal medicine, but designer babies? Are we ignoring the lessons of Nazism?[19]

It seems that artificial intelligence will unleash self-creating logics, including more virile computer viruses that mutate. As brains and computers become increasingly coupled,[20] consciousness is also likely to change, as will our relationship with it. These are important issues but must be reserved for another book. For now, I am focused only on our changing awareness of abundance, especially its bedrock position in human existence.

BUDDHISM AND CONSCIOUSNESS

Individuals and segments of society have often tried to alter whatever they thought was disturbing. But before changing anything, we need to understand the character of what is to be reconstructed, what will replace it, and whether a reformed version will result in more or fewer desirables. We often try to alter things we don't understand. Clearly, consciousness and the cosmos are out of our league. What we can change is our relatedness to these unknowns and our awareness of the presence of the cosmos and consciousness within and around us.

The best-known investigator of consciousness was Siddhartha Gautama. However, he did not set out to change it directly. He simply focused on people's suffering. He saw the downtrodden and helped them walk upright. He saw pathos and tried to alleviate it. He saw the oppressed and helped them find a liberating path. The field of psychology did not exist until 2,400 years later, but it is remarkable how many strands of the modern behavioral sciences can be found in *Buddhist* teachings and practices. Gautama strove to help people belong to life by altering the internal and external landscapes of their being, along with their cognitive processes, in particular the meanings they attached to events, emotions, thoughts, and behaviors.

Siddhartha was scientifically minded before real science existed. Medical practitioners today use the same model as he did; this is the symptom, the disease, the cause, the prognosis, and the treatment. Gautama's goal was clear: to alleviate suffering. His cure always involved remaking eight domains of the ill person's life, that individual's views, thoughts, utterances, actions, livelihood, diligence, mindfulness, and concentration. He was dedicated to altering people's actions, not their characters. He saw suffering as a symptom and the easing of pain as an indicator of an intervention's success.[21] When cure was not possible, he provided care for the needy. He also viewed aging and decay as basic existential realities to be accepted.[22]

The *Buddha's* primarily foci were the things people did that flowed naturally from their humanity and those behavioral cycles that made suffering a self-generating disease. He had five primary goals for those he was treating: (1) to change their affect if it was off base; (2) to change their thoughts if they were predicated on faulty logic; (3) to change their behavior if it was destructive to self or other; (4) to change their relationship with their feelings, thoughts, and behaviors; (5) to change the meanings that they attached to their emotions, cognitions, or actions.

Siddhartha had a secondary goal for those prepared to go deeper. He encouraged them to treat all feelings, thoughts, and behaviors as fleeting and trivial. Having seen how burdensome it was to attach significances to ordinary things his wish was for us to live perpetually in the here and now, open to the possibilities flowing to and from our external and internal landscapes. His goal was to help people build wholesome relationships with themselves, with others, with their contexts, and to have a full sense of belonging to all facets of existence.[23]

The *Buddha* lived in a time and place where the conditions of life were difficult. We too exist in a world of great complexity and are overtaxed by many unknowns. Much suffering is at the collective rather than the individual level. Groups, organizations, and societies generate many thoughts, feelings, and actions requiring consistent reparation. Suffering subsides not just when people are healed but as the larger system's thoughts, emotions, and behaviors are reconfigured. So, greater overall health is often created when interactions among systems are altered.

This is where *Buddhist* teaching helps. So many of the meanings we attach to the collective emotions and thoughts created by the interactions among groups, organizations, and communities are hollow. This emptiness is the source of much modern-day suffering. Since the dis-ease is in the collective, that is where we need to apply our treatments. When these interactions are collaboratively repaired, the parties can make appropriate and health-filling adaptations to their reformed circumstances.

The Boca case illustrates well the *Buddha's* principles. The people and the groups were not altered. Boca did not undergo psychic reprogramming. The police were not replaced or retrained. The officers were not sent to culture-sensitivity workshops. All of them continued being the same people, groups, etc., with the same instincts and attributes. But their relationships with themselves and each other altered and the meanings attached to their collective thoughts, emotions and interactions changed.

Even though only a few minor things were tweaked, a lot was re-formed. In particular a major element of collective suffering and illness in their establishment subsided greatly, as people learned how to more fully belong to themselves and to one another.

SUMMARY

We have now entered the third layer of abundance where there are many human dynamics. I have chosen to discuss three, belonging, conflict, and anxiety, which are highly interactive. While this chapter shone some light on all of them, the spotlight was primarily on belonging. That is reversed in the next chapters, where conflict and anxiety respectively are in the foreground.

The existence and maintenance of abundance are dependent on a high level of *yin-yang* functionality. In the societal domain, there are many yet-to-be-created *yin-yang-like* processes. *Belongingness* is one of them.

These are the key maxims explored in this chapter:

- The truths found in a legend are wellsprings of abundance.
- Belongingness grows as adversaries affirm their mutual angsts.
- *Here* and *there* are the same, for upon reaching *there* we are still in a *here* state.
- A legend has meaning if it resonates with the truths in us.
- Profound solutions are simple.
- Being *a part of* and *apart from* a place creates both aloneness and belongingness.
- Belonging and aloneness create each other.
- The union of aloneness and belonging leads to abundance.
- Our Self changes when we alter our relatedness to others.
- Altering the meanings we attach to thoughts and emotions increases abundance.

CHAPTER 9

COLLABORATIVE CONFLICTS

When geologists dig through earth's encrustations, they come to strata containing veins and coagulations of minerals. Upon being separated, each metal has its own unique appearance and its own energy system. Analogously, descending into the third layer of abundance we encounter the amalgam of belonging, conflict and anxiety. Our focus here is on conflict. But as with the last and the next chapter, none of these can be understood independent of its relationship with the other two.

I begin with a story about the battles between my greatest academic adversary and myself, which were relatively fruitless until a crisis hurled us onto a healthy path. No longer able to avoid working together our mutual anxieties gave us such a firm foundation that our conflicts ceased to be debilitating and became enhancing for ourselves, our peers and our graduate students. In time, our collaborative conflicts became so central to our joint modus operandi we were thoroughly bonded to one another, not because our incongruities had lessened but because we were both relating to our discords in new ways. This story ended in a manner that still takes my breath away.

Many people act as if conflict is inherently problematic. When surrounded by chaos-creating strife it is reasonable to think that the tensions among people, groups, organizations, and societies should be circumvented. In our determination to avoid conflict, it is easy to blame others for any cacophony and fail to recognize that most eruptions have their origins in our own personages, our own groups, or our own organizations. It is also hard to recognize the constructive energies that might exist if we could keep polar positions closely connected, as happens when an electric current is being created.

Conflicts between and among conditions or states of being are treated as normal when seasons of the year rotate or as dry periods come to an end with the arrival of the monsoons. In addition, nature is full of conflict-laden signals, that contribute to the critical regulators upon which the *yin-yang* adaptive process depends.

A treatise on conflict contained in one of the *Hindu* wisdom literatures offers a refreshing approach to conflict. I will use this story to reframe the value of conflict. By the conclusion of this chapter, three lessons will have been explicated: (1) Science shows that nature's creative energies result from polarities being held in close proximity long enough for the inter-connectedness inherent in their opposition to develop a new form. The same is the case in the human domain. (2) Attempts to delegitimize or eradicate naturally occurring conflicts usually drive them underground or send them to some other place. (3) Those able and willing to remain in the center of conflicts become a part of the abundance-creating process.

ADVERSARY EXTRAORDINAIRE

My first US academic position was at a large state university where I became the fifth member of an industrial/organizational psychology unit. All were white males. Jack, the most senior, and I, the most junior, were at the poles on every dimension. He chaired the department of 50 faculty and held establishment values. I was a novice cruising the fringe. Three colleagues occupied the spaces between us. When Jack and I misread one another, they bridged the gap.

I was hired to help broaden the intellectual base of this program and quickly rose to the challenge. Then I did something that created a furor. I ran a four-day retreat[1] attended by all our PhD candidates that radicalized the thinking of these scholars-in-the-making. Returning to the projects that paid their tuition, they questioned the veracity, validity, and viability of everything. Understandably, that ruffled my colleagues' feathers. A meeting of our five-person group was urgently called. Jack led the charge: "Smith, I can't believe you so quickly wrecked what we have built over many years!" He was outraged that his mentees were bullishly parroting my views in ways that undermined his authority. He tolerated my solo voice confronting orthodoxy but being clubbed by neophytes acting as if they had found the Holy Grail in a few days was too much for him!

This indictment by my most senior colleague, my supervisor, and my uber-boss demanded a rapid response. I resorted to instinct.

"Jack, it's fine for you to be angry at me about this, but I won't accept all the blame. When being recruited, I told you my approach to education and research. You said this was why you hired me! But as I have begun to do what you asked of me, you are now preparing to shut me down. I wish I'd known your real views and positions before coming from the other side of the world to join you guys. We've now hit a blip that will test our integrity. But it is not the end of our little world, unless we make it so." Blatantly playing the vulnerability card, I said, "Please recognize how destructive your rage could be. My visa has to be renewed each year. As department chair, if you even hint to Immigration and Naturalization Services that you are ambivalent about my work, they'll order me to leave the country."

The man occupying the middle spot in our five-person unit intervened, blocking a surgical scapegoating. "Wait a minute! Last week Dr. Smith got our students thinking in new ways. That is good! If we had done this, we'd feel mighty proud of ourselves. That is what a professor is supposed to do!" This led to a great conversation about what we were collectively trying to achieve, what was kosher and what was off limits.

I came to appreciate all of my colleagues anew that day, Jack in particular. He had told me what he thought and felt, explicitly declaring his own and the institution's vulnerabilities. And he made it clear that he would never punish me for expressing my thoughts, emotions, or anxieties.

As we ended, Jack declared his position: "To survive and deliver on our commitments, you, Dr. Smith, and I will have to work out how to learn from each other. But no matter how hard I listen to you, I never understand what you are saying. If it weren't for these three blokes translating for me, you could be talking Chinese. No more surprises, PLEASE! If our students change too fast, I won't be able to work with them anymore. I'll continue to support you so long as you don't conduct such radicalizing events."

I accepted this trimming of my wings, mostly out of respect for him and my peers, who felt our unit was not robust enough to ride out the perturbations any of us might intentionally or accidentally activate. However, I privately acknowledged that this would not be my long-term academic home.

Jack and I survived our initial upheavals, but we suddenly encountered several institutional earthquakes. The two men closest to me on our five-person spectrum were lured away to other places and the one nearest to Jack agreed to serve as interim dean of the graduate programs on this campus. Our shared dreams were shattered. To enable our program to survive, let alone ever thrive again, Jack and I had to collaborate.

We hunkered down, supervised many dissertations together, cotaught several courses, jointly structured research projects, and ran a multi-person enterprise on the energies of two. During our rebuilding, Jack and I brought very divergent views to every issue. In the process, we learned to treat our differences as complementary. Both of us benefited from the ways we adjusted to one another. Eventually, the long-term viability of our program was restored and became robust enough that if either or both of us were to leave, all would be fine.

Across my career I have forged significant relationships with many people who were very different from me, but none was more challenging than partnering with Jack. I valued becoming a good collaborator with a man much more senior than me who was my greatest academic adversary and who was intellectually and affectively the antithesis of me. I began my scholarly life presuming I would be the author of my own destiny. I still accept the importance of self-agency and self-responsibility. During those years, I came to recognize that all of us are like trees in a forest, each of which only exists when sustained by the hidden relationships among all the natural resources surrounding it. Biodiversity matters. Jack and I together became the epicenter of our intellectually diverse professional environment.

In time, it was right for me to move on. As my departure date approached, the sadness in our community was acute. Concerned about how to manage these emotions, Jack asked me to design and run my farewell event at our last seminar, which all graduate students and faculty attended. I proposed that we discuss the autobiographical events in our lives, which were shaping us as scholars. Several people would normally have been reticent to do such a task, but given the tender affect around my leave-taking, everyone acceded to my request.

Three decades later I recall little of what was said, but I remember almost verbatim Jack's words. He acknowledged his dislike of any activity that might stir emotions, but since it was me who had asked, he would speak his mind. The first thing he discussed was the impact of his father's death when Jack was a boy, a fact he had never revealed and which spoke volumes about his tenacious character. After identifying two other issues, he turned and spoke to me directly.

"The other defining event in my life was meeting you, Dr. Smith. Every person here knows you and I disagree on almost everything. But I have come to really appreciate you. You have led me to reconsider every value and belief I've ever held. That was hard! At times I did not like what I saw. Mostly I realized I was right all along. Today some of my values are the same. Others have changed. But now, I am clear about what is most important to me. I'm the better for that!" Looking right at me with his light-blue, penetrating eyes, he said, "You, just by the way you are, single-handedly taught me to keep reassessing who I am. And you showed me how to do it. I thank you for all you have done for me as a colleague and as a person."

Stillness filled the room. I was extremely touched. We were all awed by Jack's being so emotionally expressive.

As I was packing my books prior to my departure, he dropped by my office, making as he left a typical Jack-like quip: "It's getting to feel like a morgue around here!" I just nodded.

The last day of the semester everyone assembled to hear Jack do a run-through of a public speech he was soon to deliver. The room was arranged auditorium style. He was already at the podium as I arrived and took the only open seat, right in front, just three feet from where he was standing.

"Ladies and Gentlemen..." he began. After stating his purpose and his central thesis he told a joke. As the laughter subsided, Jack began to sway. I jumped up and caught him as he collapsed while having a massive coronary. He took his final breath in my arms. Of course, we did CPR until the paramedics arrived. But I knew with certainty that Jack's life had ended. I felt it in my chest as I held him.

His passing, at the age of 50, released waves of grief in our community. Many men, women, children, students, former mentees, colleagues from near and far gathered to remember, celebrate, and mourn. I was very grateful that I had never walled myself off from Jack, that we had done the tough emotional work to befriend each other, and that we had said our goodbyes.

To this day, several times a week I think of Jack, and my breastplate tingles a little. It still carries the tactile memory of his chest and mine in a final moment of togetherness. I am awed that I was holding Jack as he made the journey between life and death. I now know in my bones that this is a gentle passage, one to be cherished as dearly as life itself. The fact that a man who was once my nemesis ushered me into this realization makes this knowledge exceedingly special.

ELECTRIFYING ENERGIES

The more Jack and I tussled, the greater our anxiety. The more anxieties we shared, the more bonded we became. Our clashes and the attendant angst, which were often electric, strengthened our links and thrust us into deeper levels of conflict and anxiety. Our energy system was also sustaining for our students, who liked being around when he and I were functioning as a single unit, firing on all cylinders.

I valued the days we spent together, although my heart missed an occasional beat when we came close to over-adrenalizing our disputes. Jack became a companionable brother to me rather than the dismayed boss he first was.

Our mutual angst, born of our conflicts, led us to fully belong to one another and showed others that they too could create a sense of communal belonging by accepting the conflict-filled facets of existence. This conflict-anxiety-belonging nexus epitomizes the third layer of abundance.

Electricity seems an apt metaphor for collaborative combatants. Schoolchildren learn that atoms have a nucleus made of protons and neutrons along with electrons orbiting it. An electron's negative charge matches the positive charge of a proton with the number of electrons and protons in an atom usually being equal. Particles with opposite charges attract. Those with the same charge repel. Disturbing the positive-negative, proton-electron balance causes an electric current.[2] Bore a bit deeper however and electricity is an enigma. It is at the same time invisible and visible, matter and energy, a flow that can be stored, a capacity, and a measurable event, even though it has no quantity.

In the physical realm, opposites and similarities are constantly in an attraction-repulsion dance, creating currents. Likewise, the pulls and pushes of interpersonal and organizational interactions create energy, pumping positivity and negativity into relationships and workplaces.[3] That was the story of Jack and me. We bewildered ourselves and others, as we accidently created currents. Sometimes they were problematic. Mostly they were magical.

The alluring and repelling that exist in human interactions come in two forms. The pendulum in a grandfather clock and the playground swing set demonstrate the presence of a tipping point when swaying right starts to swerve left or an upward movement begins shifting downward. That is the first.

The second is when entities draw too close they may push each other away. Opposites can become and remain bonded, so long as what connects them is sufficiently adhesive to deal with the turmoil that will inevitably threaten their connections. This happens in nature, in people's psyches, in groups, in organizations, in societies. Connected countervailing forces can serve as a *yin-yang* type regulator.

At certain overheated or overcooled levels, *binding* becomes *fragmenting* and *strength* becomes *weakness*. This *yin-yang* process seems to be everywhere. An overload of *cohering, integrating, unifying* can result in *repelling, disintegrating, fragmenting*, and vice versa. People, groups, institutions are shaped by the *adhering* and the *splintering*, by the revolutions of *affixing* and *detaching*. In the specific moments of transition, this can be a nightmare signaling the onset of a scarcity. But if we are patient enough, we often find such an undoing reinforces abundance.

DEMOCRATIC AUTOCRACY AND AUTOCRATIC DEMOCRACY

In the early days, Jack and I were like warriors. If one of us yelled, "DEMOCRACY," the other screamed, "AUTOCRACY!" And then we charged with swords drawn!

These two political forms are interesting. Each operates in concert with its opposite.

Consider the USA. It uses democratic principles for national governance but not for major corporations where workers do not get to vote on the big decisions. In the USA, corporate owners can move factories and divisions to wherever they like, dismissing their workers or selling to the highest bidders their assets, including personnel. Like cattle or slaves!

National democracy, organizational autocracy! This nation espouses governance of, by, and for the people, but only in the political realm. Not for organizations!

In contrast, for decades, a single political party has ruled China, without gaining a mandate from the people. Yet it is awash with democratically governed, market-driven, free-flowing processes created and sustained by the local citizenry. While there have been many state-owned enterprises in China, history has shown that government-run Chinese businesses were no match for extra-legal, communally designed, entrepreneurial organs operating with a capitalist zeal rivaling that of the West.[4] National autocracy, organizational democracy! Plus, to the surprise of many Westerners, national socialism and local capitalism!

National democracy, organizational autocracy! National autocracy, organizational democracy! Competing complementary worlds!

The dance of centripetal and centrifugal forces seems to be as present in the sociopolitical realm as they are in physics!

Jack and I regularly gyrated around any potential polarity, with each of us trying to establish that our own take on reality was the more valid. Ultimately, we agreed to add both-and logics to our either-or thinking. I suspect this was our salvation. I did not know this at the time, but there appears to be a *yin-yang* regulator that converts either-or logic into both-and reasoning and integrates both of these logical forms.[5]

OTHERIZING BOTH THE OTHER AND THE SELF

Everyone engages in *otherizing*, that is, people treat us as an *"other"* in such invalidating ways we resort to viewing them as *others*! Philosophers even gave this process a special category, calling it dualism. *Why can't a woman be more like a man,* wailed Henry Higgins in the *My Fair Lady* drama! Why do people in different cultures have such difficulty understanding each other? Why do emotionally provoked people resort to *we-they* postures? The most painful aspect of my relationship with Jack was how we otherized each other, thereby otherizing our selves.

We all seem hard-wired to *otherize*, crafting a sense of *who we are* by using others. As infants start to distinguish between *not-me* and *me* they are beginning to live in a relational world. Seeing *other* as *other* and *self* as separate from *other* is a prerequisite to recognizing boundaries between objects and entities. Comparing *self* with *other* also builds a sense of one's abilities and attributes. For example, children race against *others* of their same age and size to determine if they are good runners; job seekers assess their employability by comparing themselves with *other* potential candidates; to monitor the flow of events, we include *others'* vantage points, map what happened in an-*other* time and consider the impact of possible outcomes on *other* parts of the world.

These social comparisons, which depend on the concept of self and other, require a difference that makes a difference, but not so much disparity that comparability is impossible.[6] Individuals and entities are perpetually making self-judgments using others as looking glasses.[7]

Despite the obvious pitfalls, what is mirrored back via the reactions of others offers a concrete starting point, even though the resultant self-constructions might be quite inaccurate.

Humans often use reflection systems selectively. A work unit can concoct an inflated sense of itself by making contrasts with only low-performing groups. A nation can pick a fight with weaker foes, thereby developing a bloated view of its own strength. If parties compare themselves only with others who are weak, it is a fallacy to conclude that the self is strong, or vice versa! We often use *others* to reach such self-deceptive conclusions.[8]

In hindsight, Jack and I otherized one another until we both learned how not to otherize.

Mercifully, when we stopped *otherizing*, we saved our *Selves* from ourselves! However, for all our days together, we were like warriors caught in the middle of battles that we jointly created. Having never found a viable exit strategy, we stayed in the middle of these kafuffles. That enabled us to hold and integrate potent polarities, a unifying place, which would never have even existed in our particular world had one of us won the war or if our duo had been splintered.

EMANCIPATING POLARITIES

Over centuries, Indian thought wove a vast array of intellectual premises into a complex tapestry that integrated its many peoples, cultures, and languages. Its main precepts are found in the traditions stemming from this land, *Hinduism, Jainism, Buddhism,* and *Sikhism.* The most prevalent today, *Hinduism* is based on a collection of texts known as the *Vedas* and the *Upanishads,* written in *Sanskrit* by anonymous sages between 1,500 and 500 BCE.

However, most people learn *Hindu* principles via epic stories, the best known being the *Bhagavad Gita*, the *Song of the Blessed One*, which is *a love song to reality, to darkness, and to luminescence, to the one true self in the core of all beings.*[9]

The *Gita* asks us to accept that everything is a manifestation of *Ultimate Reality*, which *Hindus* call *Brahman*. This is the unifying force linking everything and providing the vitality propelling all things. As with the *Tao,* the *Hindu* sense of the *transcendent* cannot be grasped by the mind or encapsulated by language. To create a sketch of *Ultimate Reality, Hindus* used mythic tales that attach simplifying shapes, identities, and names to this inferred *divine force,* while cautioning us not to treat depictions of anything as being *the* reality, not to mistake the map for the territory. The divine facet of each individual's inner core, which they named *Atman*, the *Higher Self,* is a micro-level analogy of *Ultimate Reality.* Sadly, human confusion often masks the *Braham-Atman-unity*, causing the symbol for the divinity in each being to appear distant and metaphysical. Hence, any brief but normal glimpse of the *Brahman-Atman* alignment can easily be characterized as a mystical revelation.[10]

The *Bhagavad Gita* is a treatise on life's normal polarities hidden within the psyche. It is a poetic representation of these dueling dichotomies.[11] The *Gita* reports an exchange between a warrior, Arjuna, and his charioteer, *Krishna*, who is understood to be a representation of the divine. Arjuna, who is also called the *one who has conquered sleep, the always vigilant, the awoken one,*[12] is exhausted from fighting against his own kith and kin in a protracted family war. He is about to discover that his real battles are not the external ones but the internal struggles associated with his longing for *enlightenment.*[13]

Arjuna, the warrior, craves a new level of self-realization, not because he wants spiritual clarity but because he can no longer stand the pain of being fully human. The pretend dialogue between Arjuna and his charioteer, an imaginary representation of *Krishna*, is a brawl between his inner fighter and his own Higher Self. Arjuna is in the middle of a battlefield where two sets of his relatives are trying to obliterate each other. One side is portrayed as paragons of virtue, the other as evil. Symbolically, they are the warrior's own sub-personalities, his internalizations of family members from both sides of the virtue-evil divide. The conflict is ultimately a struggle for personal authenticity, an attempt to transcend ignorance, hatred, and self-centeredness.[14]

Packaged as spiritual warfare, this is a phantom drama of the mind produced by one's ego, with the good and evil parts of it personified as virtues and vices. To absorb the meaning of their conversation, we need to keep in mind that *Krishna* and Arjuna are the same being and the tensions they work to unravel exist within everyone. This is not an historic account of a military skirmish or a fanciful spiritual fracas. It is a battle between the demonic and divine impulses in humans.[15] Using you and me as referents, *Krishna* is our respective *Higher Self*, our charioteer to whom we give the reins steering our lives.[16] Arjuna is our unbridled humanity, bone- and soul-weary from myriad futile struggles, seeking ways to simplify the complex.

Arjuna is questioning whether he should keep fighting. His real concern is *how to live* with his rival moral proclivities permanently located center stage. But he longs to be done with everything that is too disconcerting. *Krishna*, his *Higher Self*, bypasses the mind and addresses the heart, sending him the message that his cognitive paralysis is an expression of his emotions, which can only truly be dealt with in the affective realm.[17]

This veteran warrior has lost his nerve. Positioned in the midst of the opposing parties, he sees his situation clearly. Arjuna is anxious, not about slaying, per se, but about killing his kinsmen and the pointlessness of it all, even if he is successful. For the evil he has sought to banish via this war would demean everyone and forever cling to both the vanquished and the victorious.

He is filled with grief. For so long he had done his duty, encouraging the wing of the family he most identified with to engage in right conduct (*dharma)* and to exterminate the other side, the epitome of irresponsibility, fickleness, and wickedness (*adharma).* A simple response could have been *do not fight.* But that was not what *Krishna* said. Brushing aside Arjuna's sorrow, he says the real problem is his cowardice, for this warrior's heart knows that if he were to exit the scene, the result would be a bloodbath. Walking away was not an option!

Arjuna's task is to remain in the middle and learn the arts of maintaining the struggle. By keeping the battle alive, he can limit the wounding and help the ongoing polarities to continue coexisting. Delegitimizing the conflict or destroying either side would solve nothing. A warrior's work is to hold the discordant schisms in their juxtaposed positions, to delicately balance events from a middle position, and to learn the secrets of juggling overheated, clashing opposites.[18]

This exchange is between a warrior and *Krishna*, who is Arjuna's *Atman*, the divinity residing in every human. The words uttered are to be regarded as advice from the source of *Eternal Wisdom* to a potential *Awakened One*, who is caught in a false distinction between them and us, the esteemed and the maligned. *Krishna* starts by being very explicit:

- Stop thinking about preserving or killing anyone as being more or less desirable.
- Human action, no matter how noble, carries some violence and is a form of *mini-killing*.
- The death of *us*, of *our side* of the warring camps, can be as healing as slaying the opposition.
- Our viability is dependent on *letting go of* what we cling to most diligently.
- Releasing from our being whatever we cherish most is a form of *mini-death*.
- Evil is inherent in an action, not in an action's consequences.

Krishna proceeds to instruct Arjuna, in a form paraphrased below.[19] As I write and as you read, let us identify with Arjuna, the soldier, the warrior in us, and at the same time, let's be listening to the words of *Krishna*, his/our charioteer, the embodiment of his/our *Higher Self*.

Kenwyn, reader, fellow-sojourner, Arjuna, your sorrow is sheer delusion. That which never was cannot exist, and that which exists cannot cease to exist. Everything physical is transient. The Presence pervading the universe is imperishable, unchanging, beyond both "what is" and "what is not." Our bodies come to an end, but the vast embodied Self is ageless, fathomless, and eternal. This Self, having come to be will never not-be. Just as the self throws out old clothes and puts on new ones, the Self discards its used bodies and enters new ones. The Self is vast, perfect, all pervading, calm, immoveable, timeless. Do not grieve over what is inescapable.

Before birth, beings are unmanifest. Between birth and death, they are manifest. At death, they are unmanifest again. This Self, dwelling in every body, does not die.[20]

Everyone is asked to develop ways to be above dichotomies, to be equally indifferent to happiness and suffering. Arjuna was not told to avoid action but to act always *as if* he were neutral about what happens.[21] All of us are directed to do the tasks associated with our roles and to accept that every outcome is the product of many contributions.[22] But everything is to be done with integrity, which means acting without seeking gain for the self.[23] The *Gita* says we are accountable for what we do, but we are not entitled to claim credit for the results. The spirit with which we do a task determines its authenticity.[24]

What exquisite advice this warrior got from his *Higher Self*! Arjuna initially faced a first order *suffering*, the conflict among his own sub-personalities coalesced as warring camps that led him into the battle and to fight on behalf of the better faction. But each opposing party's perspective had validity, and both polarities were a part of him. This was second-order *suffering*, and it was harder to handle than the pain that initially caused the battle. He wanted to quit, but there was no exit. His only option was to stay, to keep alive the conflicts, to coexist with them and the attendant discord. This was third-order *suffering*. What a strange thought, that primitive suffering can be redeemed by more advanced suffering!

The *Gita* asks every person to dwell in the middle of our internal conflicts, to heed the *Buddhist* notion of *harmony being controlled or synchronized dissonance*. Science shows that nature's creative energies result from polarities being held in close proximity long enough for the interconnectedness inherent in their opposition to be released as a fresh manifestation. How stunning and magnificent that over 2,500 years ago, before the birth of rationalism and the scientific method, a poet's insights about the human psyche presaged 21st-century physicists: *that which constrains, expands; that which limits, enhances; that which is scarce, is abundant.*

SUMMARY

Continuing the thesis previously proposed, that abundance requires the balancing of the *yin-yang* dynamic, in this chapter we spotlighted the role of conflict. The most glaring feature of conflict is that it is inherent in all things. It also has the potential to dominate the interactions among objects, energies and anything that flows. The argument that conflict is natural, good, and indispensable is counterintuitive for most people. That is in large part because conflict appears to create anxiety and anxiety can easily be made into a source of suffering. Hence, we attempt to eliminate suffering by getting rid of conflicts. But in doing so, we rob the *yin-yang* balancing process of an essential tool, which leads to the very scarcity conflict-assuaging activities are attempting to avoid.

On several counts, we have this backward. Another option is to accept conflicts for what they are, inherent contradictions, diverse perspectives, normal tussles between preserving what is and enabling the emergence of what-might-be. Then the conflicts that result from negating what is in the natural order of things would lead to less secondary conflicts and less suffering. By striving to outlaw those conflicts we make them self-fueling. As the Arjuna story displayed, trying to banish the inevitable recreates the conflicts we want to eradicate. Then we end up having to manage secondary and tertiary conflicts that are growing more taxing.

The main lessons emerging from this chapter are:

- Conflicts assist the functionality of the abundance fulcrum.
- Conflicts with others arise out of our own internal clashes.
- Our biggest conflict is *how to live* with our own inner contradictions.
- Accepting our inner conflicts creates a sense of belonging.
- When we *otherize others*, we are also *otherizing* our*selves*.
- Ceasing to *otherize* self and others lessens *we-they-ness*.
- *Splintering* and *adhering* animates the *yin-yang* regulators.
- Centripetal and centrifugal forces help sustain abundance.
- *Yin-yang* dynamics give *either-or* logics a *both-and* form.
- Abundance is the unification of the discordant.

CHAPTER 10

ANXIETY'S HIDDEN TREASURES

Throughout this book, we have been exploring what makes for an effective abundance-scarcity regulator. Good governors seem to exist in nature, but many still need to be discovered or created in the human and sociopolitical realm. The components of the third strata such as those discussed here are a consequence of and a contributor to the calibration of just-enoughness and not-too-muchness. This chapter centers on anxiety and its ties to belonging and conflict.

To contextualize this discussion, I begin with a brief reference to the cosmic entity called a black hole. Even those of us with little knowledge of this strange astronomical beast often refer to an awful situation as a black hole. Several of our stories, such as Boca, Jack, and Arjuna, are about potential black-holes-in-the-making, as is the one that opens this chapter. But as already discussed, when things are packed into small spaces, lots of energy can get unleashed. Likewise, with psyches and communities!

What is a black hole, a term that entered our vocabulary in the 1960s?[1] As a large star expires, there is an explosion that scatters debris and leaves behind a cold remnant where fusion can no longer occur. Normally a star's nuclear fusion produces sufficient outward-propelling energy to offset the inward-directed gravity generated by its own mass.[2] Without fusion, this large gravitational force lacks a countervailing opposition. Like all large celestial objects, black holes pull matter and energy into them when other planets or light cruise too close.[3]

Where nothing can escape a black hole's clutches, there is an imaginary zone around it called the *event horizon*.[4] Just outside the *event horizon*, all objects gyrate in the same direction, but at a certain point very close to the black hole, the rotation flips and goes in the opposite direction. Is this a cosmic *yin-yang* dynamic at work? From then on, to remain stationary, the outer and inner rotations must go faster than the speed of light![5] An expiring star internally shrinks to zero volume, becoming infinitely dense and all light gets trapped within its orbit.[6]

As a star dies, time at its surface slows down, relative to clocks elsewhere. When time comes to a standstill, the star stops disassembling.[7] However, contrary to what normally happens with entropy, the decaying affects its area, not its volume. This gives it a holographic form, with the happenings going on inside it being made visible on its surfaces. To scientists' chagrin, the dynamics within a black hole operate on laws of physics that are the opposite of those that fit the world outside![8]

When discussing knowledge development, it is important to remember that although science helps us appreciate some principles of existence, life is not knowable by studying only galaxies, planets, molecules and cells. [9] Everything we claim to know is subjective, for every organism's realities are based on associations among its sensing systems and its cognitive apparatus. That does not mean scientific findings are irrelevant or should be discarded. To the contrary! While the knowledge we create may not reduce our bewilderment, it reveals the vastness of our ignorance, thereby increasing our humility, a very valuable gift.

It is counterintuitive to think of anxiety as increasing abundance. While some see it as a black hole, anxiety serves a useful function, an idea I hope we are now ready to consider.

In the foundation of the three main monotheistic faith traditions, *Judaism, Christianity*, and *Islam*, is found the story of a man named *Abraham*, which has been retold for 4,000 years. Over the generations, new meanings have been attached to this narrative. I will discuss one that is often overlooked, Abraham's discovery of a major link between anxiety and consciousness. If we take the Abrahamic logic one further step, we can see how the anxiety-consciousness nexus leads to more abundance.

DEFLATION AND SILVER LININGS

Upon completing my graduate education, I accepted a position at Melbourne University. My first course was with 50 MBA students who were my age. I assumed they would be keen learners and would appreciate an overseas-educated Aussie as their instructor. I was wrong on both counts!

I poured my heart into preparing my opening class and appreciated their attentiveness. As I ended, however, one man sneered, "What latest new-fangled American book did that garbage come from!" I calmly stated, "I used many sources. Each class I'll give you handouts of my materials." Another guy beefed up the aggression. "All your examples are American. If you're going to teach here, give us Aussie cases!"

Nipping this in the bud, I replied, "Fair enough. We are adjourned for today!" That was the high point of our first weeks together. By midsemester, I hit rock bottom, doubting if I had the constitution for this profession. I was awfully out of sync with these students.

Despite my plummeting spirits, after two months I requested them to evaluate our progress to date. We were going down in flames, and I needed to know why. Although dreading what might be unleashed, I threw down the gauntlet. "Someday you may be in a situation like mine. This course is going badly. Daily I ask what am I doing wrong? Why are your reactions to the material and me so hostile? Do you feel coerced to take this required course? Soon I will be giving you feedback on your papers, and I'd like you to reciprocate by addressing seven questions. You'll see they range from 'what is Kenwyn doing that aids or hinders your learning' through to 'what could you do to make this course a success for yourselves and your peers.' Please do this assessment in your newly formed project groups and be ready at our next class to report out on all seven questions."

When they presented their assessments, all groups addressed only one topic: what is wrong with the instructor! Their criticisms were endless and vitriolic! I took the barrage as best I could, but my energies were seeping out of me. Their critiques, however, did hint that they wanted things to change but felt powerless to act. I wondered if I should halt this exercise, but I let it continue. Having opened Pandora's box, I knew the responsibility for dealing with it was squarely on my shoulders.

Many complaints were valid, but I wondered if they were projecting onto me their feelings about past teachers and former disappointments. My inner reactions to them were so extreme I resolved to listen intently. Their aches echoed my own reactions to teachers cramming learning down our throats. Even as undergrads, we were drilled not to express our own ideas, to consider only scholars' views on any subject! I had craved for ideas to be *companions* rather than *things* to be regurgitated! Soon I saw the double bind I had constructed. I was trying to get my students to be creative! But maybe they were thinking that expressing anything except the teacher's view of the *right answer* would lead to being punished. I had argued that there are no correct ways to manage organizational complexities, that it is best to take actions based on their own synthesis of the available evidence. No wonder I was an enigma! My approach was sending their anxiety through the roof!

By the end of their reports, I had a hypothesis: if their sense-of-self-as-learners had been damaged in the past, the more I challenged them to think creatively, the more inner resistance they felt. I had no idea if this was accurate, however my musings suggested a potential path to take. But first I privately pondered whether I had the adequate inner resources to manage what was ahead and if my theorizing was robust enough to help explain the troubles we were experiencing. Although this was probably mere hubris, my answer to both questions was yes.

Determined to let them know that although wounded I could still function, I said, "Your comments hurt, but I appreciate your truthfulness. I hope the small portion of the task you did can be a basis for new learning. But I am wondering why no group did the actual assignment."

"What do you mean, we didn't do what was asked of us?" one man said in a respectful tone.

"All of your groups focused on only one question, what's wrong with the instructor. You were to address seven issues, not just one," I said empathetically. "If this was an exam with many questions and you only completed one, you'd expect to fail. If your boss gave your workgroup several tasks and you did just one, you'd be instructed to repeat them or to look for a new job."

I asked, "Did you consciously decide to do only a fraction of what was required? Or was this an out-of-awareness oversight? If it was the latter, you were likely caught up in a classic group dynamic.

But if you elected not to respect the demands of the authority figure, in this case me, what actions did you expect to evoke? You are well aware of the instructor-student power differentials in a university, so what do you anticipate my next move would be? Were your actions purposeful or only a way to vent? Please discuss these issues together during this week. Power struggles like what you and I are now experiencing will be the theme for our next gathering!"

Within days, half the class had contacted me. They began by saying they had beaten me up badly and hoped I was okay! My response was "I'm still reeling, but overall I am fine." Many then asked me to help them with a problem at work or a relationship conflict. During these chats, they revealed their wish for things to alter. Next class we explored the group and organizational dynamics operative during the previous weeks. The students, no longer clammed-up or cagy, joined in forthright exchanges. I asked them to commit to having our sole purpose be advancing our shared understanding of the content the course was designed to address. They debated this openly. Soon it was obvious everyone was ready to make such a pact.

The last half of the semester was as spectacular as the first half was torturous. These students let me become their guide and many seized their own self-educating role. We began an optional breakfast seminar at my home every Wednesday morning. Most of them came to several of these sessions. I cooked piles of pancakes and French toast as they discussed a designated topic.

My rookie term as a faculty member began with two months of lows. It concluded with students and teacher being transported to a place that rebuilt our confidence in the learning process.

SIFTING THROUGH THE RUBBLE

There are many professionals who can recognize when parties are heading into clashes caused by disconnects between different versions of reality, organizational structures and groups in conflict.

The first step of an intervention is to identify the primary anxieties giving rise to the basic conflicts that escalate and produce secondary anxieties, which generate secondary conflicts, etc. After a few rotations of the anxiety-conflict wheel, anxieties can easily get concretized and become explicit fears, which are then expressed as threats, otherizing, we-they stances, blaming, and microaggressions. With every revolution of the anxiety-conflict cycle, the *yin-yang* process becomes increasingly misaligned. However, such *yin-yang* disruptions are filled with abundance-enhancing energies if that anxiety-conflict spiraling can be interrupted and redirected.

Initially I did not notice the anxiety-conflict nexus paralyzing my MBA students. I will walk through the evolution of that anxiety escalation, hoping that readers will be able to recognize when you are in such situations. The secret is when you most want to squelch anxiety, embrace it!

Returning to Melbourne during my age-thirty transition,[10] I was worried about whether my international perspectives would be of value in my homeland. I was eager to fit in, to belong. But I wanted to belong only in places that I respected. One of my start-up mistakes was accepting a higher academic rank than I deserved. Hoping to justify this status, I entered my first MBA class like a hotshot. Even if my ideas were fine, my demeanor was off-putting, which my students sniffed and flung back in my face.

Included in this miscalculation was my insistence that there were no right answers to thorny managerial problems. That led to the students concluding that "if this instructor does not have any solutions to the problems we face, why is he here and why should we listen to him!" That was one side of the anxiety equation. The other side, as already discussed, is that genuine learning occurs only on the boundary between what we know and what we don't know. Hovering on that brink as we try to learn new things is anxiety producing.

During their schooling, these MBA candidates would have been tracked into classes reserved for the best students. In that era, 3 percent of Australian teens were admitted to university, and two-thirds of them failed along the way! So, my students were among the 1 percent of their generation to earn a bachelor's degree. They had succeeded in settings, which spoon-fed them knowledge that they had to reproduce at exam time.

My claims about the need to be creative came across as belittling their former successes, thereby breeding a first-order version of anxiety. My decree that there are no correct answers created a second-order anxiety, and so forth. I had also made this worse by stressing that the most valuable learning occurs when we are in a not-knowing state, where ambiguity, amorphousness and anxiety reside.

Alas, I had not built a context where sharing one's ignorance could be affirmed. Nor had I built an adequate container for their anxiety. I had thrown them into an ocean of uncertainty. Their anxiety was debilitating them. And I was exacerbating it!

CREATING NEGATIVISM

There was one additional problem. During their education, these students had mastered the double negative game, which has within it a pernicious anxiety escalator. This is how it operates. The otherizing discussed in the last chapter entangles everyone in the binds of negation. *Not* and *no* have several meanings, which are often used in confusing ways. Not can signify absence, such as in "she is *not* here." That is clear. But what does it mean to say something like "you are *not* me, and I am *not* you?" Such a colloquialism is so familiar we know what it means. However, when the rules of grammar are applied to such a statement, it is logically absurd. What happens when the *not* is a negation of the pronoun *you* or *me*? There are oodles of objects, creatures, people, entities in the category *not-me* and *not-you*. In reality, *not-me* is everything other than me. To imply that not-*me* or not-*you* is everything other than *me* or *you*, is a mixing of logical types,[11] producing a vacuous utterance.

The difficulty of negation is clear when a schoolboy complains, *I learned nothing today*, or when Alice in Wonderland claims that *I see nobody on the road.* These statements evoke the retorts, *Young man, you must be very smart to learn no-thing*, and *Alice, you must have powerful eyes if you are able to see no-body.* The negation is meant to be of the verb, as in *I do NOT see* anybody, and I did *NOT learn* anything. Negating the object, the noun, implies her eyes are capable of seeing *no-thing* and he can learn *no-thing*. This shift of the *negation* from the verb to the noun occurs frequently. However, it moves the negation, which is an attribute of the speaker's actions and makes it into an attribute of the one being spoken to or about.[12]

Confusing the *not* of negation and the *not* of absence is problematic. The *not* in "A is *not present*" is a radically different *not* from the ones in the statement "A is *not not*-A," which posits that A and *not*-A are in a structural relationship of negation.[13]

Things get very muddled when *not* is used to negate something already negated. In the human realm, *negation* and *affirmation* work differently than in mathematics: a *plus* multiplied by a *plus* produces a *plus*; *plus* multiplied by *minus* results in a *minus*; *negating* a *negative* creates a *positive*. That is not the case in a sociopsychological realm. If I am happy and something shatters my happiness, I am *unhappy*. But *negating* my *unhappiness* does not make me *happy*. It makes me *mega-unhappy*, depressed.

Intellectually or emotionally *negating a negative* generates negative squared, *negativism*. When trapped in such *negativism*, we see virtually *all things* as negative. Every thing, person, and situation looks awful. But we fail to notice that others appear that way not because of what the other is like but due to the negativism lodged in the eye or the mind of the beholder! A depressed person does not overcome a malady by fighting against it, for negating negativism is negative cubed. Oddly, healing melancholia starts with affirmations, even if the only affirmable is the gloom shrouding us.[14]

Always making judgmental statements about others and always negating is data about the speaker. The less confident we are about our own intellectual capabilities the more likely we are to criticize (*negate*) another's incompetence (*non*-competence). We can even be brilliant at critiquing, using disdain of other to mask our personal anxiety and our self-generating negativism. However, saying someone else is a buffoon does not make the critic into a genius!

Most people see anxiety as a negative condition and fight against it. Before proceeding, I want to acknowledge there are people genuinely suffering from anxieties who rightly need psychiatric and/or pharmacological help. However, with the garden-variety anxiety located in the learning process attempts to get rid of anxiety is a double negative. And it does not work. Doubling down on anxiety generates fears, which in turn produce more intractable conflicts. And if that escalation goes too far, it leads to the kind of war Arjuna was fighting.

There is one further facet of anxiety that has to be identified. Most theories about the development of people, groups, and institutions can be characterized as occurring in stages. We tend to study the continuities found within the stages but not the discontinuities occurring during the actual transition. Every transition is an ending and a coming into being, a death and a birth. It is the void between what previously was and what will be. Like a violent storm or a sunrise, this morphing process is hard to capture in words.

What did our MBAs go through in their transitions from being one kind of a learner to another? Or what is the inner experience of anyone going from a single to a partnered state, from being childless to becoming parents, upon being widowed? These are big questions addressed long ago via the legendary story of Abraham, which will soon enter the scene. But first, a brief interlude!

Is there any resting place where we can be renewed in the midst of anxiety's ever-present cauldron? Is there any relationship between abundance and angst? The answer is *yes* to both queries. It may seem complex but is quite simple. Treat anxiety as an ally, not as an adversary!

Here is another take on the Arjuna story. One set of his relatives can be viewed as the coagulation of all his anxieties, the other the aggregate of his raging conflicts. Arjuna says to his charioteer, "*Krishna*, I cannot remain in the midst of all this anxiety and conflict. I do not belong here. I want this struggle to end. Tell me what to do." *Krishna* says, "This is exactly where you belong, right in the middle of these internal conflicts and anxieties of yours. Accept and learn to love both the conflict and the anxiety. They are essential parts of you. Befriend them. They are your allies, your supporters. Then even in your loneliness you will find that you belong both *here* and *anywhere* you go. Your anxieties and your conflicts will always travel with you. They will be beside you. They are your luminescence and your shadow!"

ABRAHAM AND ANXIETY

For a long time, philosophers have discussed the importance of trust, faith, belief, learning, healing, generosity, gratitude, loneliness, belonging, and conflicts, all of which contribute to knowing our inner selves and our external world.[15] Such knowledge usually comes into being via an *awakening*, which may appear as a blinding light. Or it can grow imperceptibly. It can be a mere fork in the road, a minor detour, or a bold U-turn.

An *awakening* is a call to action. The *call* is to us, but it is not about us. It is a summons to serve others. Sacrificially. Rather than offering a return on investment, its beneficence profits others. An *awakening* asks us to let go of all we cling to and to embrace what we are ignoring. It invites us to become cocreators of the possibilities tucked inside our own and others' dreams waiting for a catalyst to help nascent aspirations become reality.

The story of *Abraham* is central to the three main monotheistic faith traditions. They each view him to be their spiritual founder. A credulity-stretching account of his life surfaced in the Middle East about 4,000 years ago and was orally passed from generation to generation, until Hebrew writing was invented.[16]

Obviously there were no journalists or cameras recording the life of this man, and for ages scholars have been distressed that there is not any way to establish if this narrative is true. In my view, that is a rather trivial concern. A far more important question is *why has this story been told over and over again for four millennia*? What truths are hidden inside this mythic account that have led generations to keep repeating it?

Before plunging into Abraham's adventure, we need to recognize that long ago our ancestors had only a cyclical view of events: the sun rises and sets; ocean waves repetitively roll in and recede; seasons rotate in a predictable pattern; tomorrow becomes another yesterday; rains come and go capriciously; droughts and pestilences punctuate normalcy.[17] This take on reality changed when time became a part of human consciousness, which enabled the sequencing of events. That gave birth to history.

Now we can think about the past fading, wonder whether our present-day activities will be seen as trivial or seminal in the future, and can pass onto our progeny pictures of former events. How did people who saw life as only cyclical acquire a linear perspective? What might have been going on for those living through this transition that went from no awareness of *before* and *after* to a form of consciousness that carries time in its core?

Enter the scene, Abraham! Briefly, this is the story.[18]

Rooted in the land of his ancestors, a man named Abram, who was married to Sarai, chose to listen to a voice in his head, which he interpreted as a divine call that he should heed. It had three elements: "leave your home and move to an unidentified place; if you faithfully follow this directive, although you and your wife are old and childless, you will become the father of a great and highly unique nation; and upon reaching your destination, you will receive a new persona."

This proposition confronted Abram with many thorny issues: "Is the destination real or merely an imaginary place? Searching for the unknown, should we head north, south, east, or west? How will we know when we have arrived? Will the trip take a month or centuries? How long will it be before the first harvest, a year or a decade? Will we ever know if this *call* is anything more than an untethered thought echoing through my mind's hollow caverns?"[19]

Setting aside such disarming ambiguities, Abram and his extended family rounded up their livestock and started walking, without any roadmap, leaving behind only dusty footprints. Abram and Sarai confronted many obstacles as they stumbled along their ambiguous path and were surprised when told they were to change their names to *Abraham* and *Sarah*. This was a journey fraught with danger that led Abraham to shed his peace-loving philosophy, become a covert operative, and a fierce warrior. He won so many battles he was seen as a hero, which gave him legitimacy to continue on his way.[20] This trek, dominated by banal chores, brutal skirmishes, and brief moments of clarity, turned Abraham into a visionary. He had to dream big because his people's sagging spirits constantly needed to be bolstered by the idyllic futuristic images he had constructed. Abraham did appreciate, however, that it would take generations to know whether the long-term benefits of his choices outweighed the heavy short-term costs.

Ironically, the journey was actually reshaping Abraham. On the road, he grew into a transitional being, a person with a foot in two worlds, two psychic conditions, the recollections of his former existence plus his cravings for and curiosities about what lay ahead.

He had been promised that upon arrival at the new place he would be a new person. But was this a new physical place or a new way of locating his being in whatever place he was physically occupying? Surprisingly, the promised change had been subtly occurring during the journey. While meandering across foreign territories, he morphed into a man living in the empty spaces between the *there and then* of the past, the *here and now* of the present, and the unknown *there and then* of the future.

Before even reaching their new home, Abraham had *become both a literal and a spiritual immigrant*.[21] It was this recalibration of his essence that constituted the real fruit of his relocation.

Abraham's *new way of being in the world* would ultimately have greater significance than the land his clan came to occupy.

And the real treasure he bequeathed to the future was the discovery that shifting time from its irreversible circularity makes it possible for people to progress, to have their own personal histories, to give their own lives unique significance.[22]

This was a birthing story. Abraham had brought to life the concept of individuality, that each person can have a differentiated self, with a distinctive identity. No wonder it kept being retold.

The Abraham narrative has many historic consequences, such as his two sons, Isaac and Ishmael, whose lives supposedly led to the creation of a bifurcated Israel and Islam. However, the lesson contained in the Abraham story I wish to highlight is that although a perturbation may arrive with sudden clarity, the journeying phase of an awakening demands patience and might require months or millennia to take shape. Such an elongated process stimulates anxiety that cannot be brushed aside or banished.

Having begun this trek, Abraham had to accept that everything henceforth was uncertain, that tomorrow would not necessarily be like yesterday. From then on anxiety was going to be Abraham's ever-present companion, for he had become a perpetual sojourner.

Perhaps *the anxiety activated by the mere idea of having to migrate* is the space nomadic spirits are called to enter! Or maybe the real reason for moving is to catalyze and crystallize the inner anxieties needing to be embraced. Exiting *familiar territory* and going to a *foreign land* may not even require physical movement. It could be done directly by just entering our inner anxieties.

While wrestling with ambiguity, while searching for the right direction, one is drawn to simultaneously look backward and forward. "Should I go or stay? Is my leave-taking temporary or permanent? Can present ties be retained or must I sever everything, making a return impossible? Who and what will I take with me, or should I discard everything and go alone?" Living perpetually on the boundary between what-is and what-could-be puts us in the void betwixt clarity and confusion.[23] Accepting that the future is unknowable, recognizing there is no turning back, knowing that staying put is no longer tenable starts an action-packed period. In part, this is because the message *it is time to leave* comes as a clear clarion call and in part because movement of any kind seems anxiety assuaging. Abraham's story symbolizes that the present contains echoes of the past, that what we are doing right now shapes the future, that each moment is full of fresh potentialities, that living in the *here and now* can help to heal past wounds.

Buddhists teach that psychic turmoil is present in all renewal, that whatever torments us can be sources of inner contentment, that life is more than the dirt and drudgery of survival. They also claim that the greatest significances stream from a sphere beyond our comprehension, from some *un-nameable source*, from an *infinite intelligence.* Maybe our encounters with anxiety help us to make a companion out of the polarities populating our disorientations.

The main issue for Abraham turned out to be less about where his descendants would settle and more about how his actions helped transform his own inner and outer conditions. The decision to leave familiarity led him to embrace the yet-to-be-discovered roots sprouting within him. Upon making that shift, he was ushered into a period of great generativity. His legacy was to show us all how to accept the plethora of promises and gifts planted in us at our origins.[24]

The *Abraham* and *Buddha* archetype came from the same psycho-spiritual space. Before reaching the desired territory, Abraham entered those parts of the self that the *Buddha* also later discussed. Our inner sanctum is filled with soul-affirming whispers coming from our *Higher Self*: everything elusive, unattainable, seemingly beyond reach is already within us, waiting to be acknowledged, nurtured and released.[25] So we do not need to follow Abraham or the *Buddha* to be like Abraham and the *Buddha*, for they are already in us. We all have everything we need to become fully who we are, to create our own authentic character.[26]

To release the full force of our fruitfulness, we begin by entering our inner emptiness, the place where one is a stranger even to one's self. And there, in the most unfamiliar place, in our most alone world, we find our inner refugee, our compliment, our inner companion, the one who makes us no more a stranger anywhere. From then on, all the promises of once unreachable destinations are perpetually with us, no matter where we go, as portable as the human spirit.[27]

An awakening also makes us aware of our limitations, the magnitude of the tasks ahead and our sense of inadequacy to address what confronts us.[28] Most paralyzing is the realization that what is unleashed will shape future generations in ways we can never know in our own lifetime. However, we act anyway, trusting that the cumulative positives that will come from what is being birthed will outweigh the aggregated negatives. In a way there is no option but to trust what cannot be seen and to have faith in what does not yet exist! It is the taking of those very actions that makes the future.[29]

SUMMARY

In this chapter, we have explored anxiety, drawing to an end our discussion of what I have called the third strata of the abundance phenomenon. Abundance is in ascendency when the *yin-yang* regulators are fully functional. And the anxieties we experience in regular life are tied to the rheostats that give rise to abundance, that delicate balance of just-enoughness and not-too-muchness.

The anxieties we have been discussing are those that get expressed primarily at the individual level. However, we are all part of many collective processes and the anxieties we experience often are not just those that well up from within us. Many flow into us from others who are too overwhelmed by their own struggles or who are trying to repress their emotions because they are not adequately equipped to deal with them at that time. We often carry anxiety on each other's behalf. This is most visible in families when a parent is filled with anguish over a child who is suffering from unmanageable inner turmoil. We will never truly know in our lifetime the collective impact of our actions or inactions. But, as Reinhold Niebuhr reminded us, things worth doing are never achieved in a single lifetime.[30]

These are the main themes discussed in this chapter:

- Abundance is a facet of the mysterium that is knowable.
- Enlightenment arises as we recognize how little we know.
- N*egating negatives* creates *negativism*, an abundance sinkhole.
- Unacknowledged anxieties become concretized as fears.
- The more anxiety we can tolerate, the more abundance we can experience.
- Treating anxiety as an ally sustains abundance.
- We are always migrating from a past *there and then* to a new *there and then*.
- Anxiety is present in the birthing of all things, including abundance.
- To be like Abraham affirm the *Abraham* already in us.
- Abundance is in the ground of our being.

Conclusion

The Next Stepping-Stone

As we navigate our way through this yet-to-be-named renaissance, it is obvious we need an economic system based on abundance **and** scarcity, rather than scarcity alone. However, we first have to construct a shared sense of what we mean by abundance, one that is integrated with nature's ways of functioning. This book is my beginning contribution to this enterprise.

In the first few chapters, I argued that abundance, just-enoughness, not-too-muchness is based on three foundational elements, trust, faith, and belief. As Yuval Harari pointed out in his 2015 book, *Sapiens,* the economics based on scarcity relies on these same three principles. Momentarily, I will offer a synopsis of his views. His treatise shows how elevating economics is when operated with integrity and how devastating it is when corrupted.

The second domain I have called the level of fluidity. Abundance is not a static process. It is like our body's bloodstream, constantly circulating between centers and peripheries. Two concepts used to illustrate this facet of abundance are streams of generosity and rivulets of gratitude. To date, economics has focused mainly on amounts, with inadequate attention to issues of flow. This is evident in the perpetual problem of the over-resourced being financially obese, while those residing in under-resourced settings are wrestling with economic malnutrition. I think major advances in economics will occur when we start seeing it as society's circulatory energy system, which like electricity can flow not just to and through businesses and established sociopolitical organs but also to all the world's hinterlands.

The third domain consists of the human processes being constantly shaped by the *yin-yang-abundance* regulators. I focused on three: belonging, conflict, and anxiety. Unfortunately, economics has yet to develop some essential rheostats. It lacks any compassion for those who are made into collateral damage during endless economic wars and it does not have any internal moral rudder. In addition, economics is still predominantly based upon and depends on national law.[1] That is a problem. Globalization is currently based primarily on economics, which means we need a solid foundation of global law upon which it can rest. That body of law does not yet exist, which means the present global order is built upon some rather flimsy structures.

At the same time Einstein was developing his *theory of relativity*, which I see as the start of this yet-to-be-named epoch we are in, Mohandas Gandhi began raising his voice. In 1909, his provocative book calling for *Home Rule* of India was published. His message was unmistakable: *it is time for colonialism to end.* Over the ensuing decades, one version of colonialism faded as the chains shackling scores of so-called underdeveloped nations were snapped. However, Gandhi was equally invested in decolonizing the mind, a change far more complex than altering nations' behaviors. He was calling for a radical tweaking of human consciousness. Gandhi's life ended before most people recognized that aspect of his sociopolitical agenda. It is with us today, however. Casting off our oppressive systems of thinking is an integral part of the current re-formation we are participating in and witnessing.

Standing on the first abundance stepping-stone this book has laid out it is now possible to glimpse the next foothold. If we could ask

Gandhi what we could do to give abundance its rightful place in our lives, I think he would say: first, reestablish our ties to nature; second, reform economics; and third, return trust, faith, and belief to the people, where they rightly belong.

Inviting us to embrace nature's ways, Gandhi might point to Satish Kumar's (2002) book *You Are, Therefore I Am: A Declaration of Dependence*, especially his call to **"Be Like the Sun."**

As the sun rises, it does not assert today it will banish darkness.
    The sun is always still.
        Yet its stillness makes the world go around.
            It is totally neutral and detached.
                It does not control or dictate.
                    It just is.

The sun is not responsible for good or evil acts.
    It makes the cows graze,
        The birds sing,
            The merchants open their shops,
                The farmers plow their fields.

In the light of the sun a person may read a good or trivial book.
    One may help a neighbor.
        Another may commit murder.
            If some people sleep late,
                The sun does not force them to wake up.
                    It is enough that it exists.

By its actions the sun says that light is its nature.
　To be is to shine.
　　Even when it is dark here,
　　　The sun is shining on the other side of the Earth.
　　　The sun shines all the time,
　　　　Although we never notice it is working.

The sun is the perfect state of being, rather than doing.
　The sun does not have light.
　　It is light.
　　　The sun does not do good.
　　　It is good.

Be like the sun.

THE COIN OF THE REALM: MONEY, TRUST, MUTUALITY, AND FICTION

Second, Gandhi would ask us to end the colonizing actions of economic theories and practices. While economics has contributed greatly to human advancement, it has also *enslaved us all*, including the uber-wealthy! Almost everything we have and do is now commoditized and commercialized. Alas, as we labor each day, we are measured by the economic value we add to the system. The new economics needs to be predicated on nature's ways rather than the form of manipulative scarcity humans invented. And it needs to cease enslaving anyone!

Yuval Harari offers us a very thoughtful perspective on the evolution of the monetary system and economics, which is summarized in the next few pages.

A surface sign of scarcity, of wealth, or of abundance is the amount of money and the assets one has. In this regard, money is a symbol. The meaning of any symbol is dependent on its relationship with what it symbolizes. Money's utility is evident in purchasing essentials like food. But when there is no food due to famine, floods, earthquakes, pestilence, the value of money is zero.

At another level, money is also a symbol of something amorphous but highly significant, *trust*. Hunter-gatherers bartered face-to-face and did not need money. Giving a handful of carrots to a neighbor carried an implied reciprocity. It would be paid in the future with a bag of grain or with help fixing a hut. In such face-to-face settings, *trust* and *mutuality* were the coin of the realm. Betrayal was unthinkable, for it destroyed the trust needed for subsequent exchanges.

Money appeared when *strangers* had to *trust* one another. Anything that helped to codify the agreed-upon value of exchanged goods sufficed, such as seashells or castoff bits of leather, which could be used as an IOU. Although such artifacts had no inherent value, they made agreements easy to recall. When something worth 40 seashells was exchanged for one valued at 20 shells, the imbalance would be rectified in a later transaction. Such a pact had meaning only for the interacting parties who jointly created it. This was how the coin system developed. It was based on the *mutual trust* enshrined in the minds of the collaborators. This socio-commercial idea led to a simple coin swapping structure that existed in many places for a few thousand years.[2]

Initially a coin was a mere symbol of a relationship, which seemed desirable because everyone else also wanted it. That is when money turned into a medium of exchange, enabling any object to become a different thing. A bunch of bananas could be switched into a bucket of lentils. Money also developed into a method to store wealth. Excess grain stowed in a barn rotted. But if the surplus was sold and converted into coins small enough to stash in a pouch, accumulating money became possible. That made the actual exchange into a symbol of transformation.[3]

Money started as an idea, an artifact of human imagination. At the beginning, it was not a thing. It was a *symbol of trust*, a psychological construct existing only in the mind. But as this symbol of trust began to spread, it generated *networks based on mutual trust*. The logic? Because people *believed* in it and increasingly used coins to exchange goods or services, a *circle of trust* grew larger and ultimately included complete strangers, which significantly increased its utility.[4] Of course, trust existed alongside the possibility of mistrust, for all parties had the potential to act in an untrustworthy way.

About 5,000 years ago, to ensure that mutual trust would not get eroded, money became an object imbued with an inherent value. The initial coin was barley money, the base unit being a sila, about a liter. Silas of barley were used at the market places and to pay wages. However, it was difficult to cart large quantities of grain over long distances. That is what gave rise to portable coins, made with specified amounts of copper, bronze, nickel, silver, gold and imprinted with an official insignia signifying the value of the metal in it. By 100 CE, markets were using coins sanctioned by communities a thousand miles away. That gave rise to an expanded *system of mutual trust*, a phenomenon that was remarkably effective, despite its share of catastrophes. Across 3,000 years coins morphed into what now exists.[5]

In general, economic development was propelled by and enabled the rise of empires, the establishment of diverse political structures, along with advances in science and technology.[6]

This is the bottom line about money: (1) while being the primary building block of economics, money is actually a figment of humans' imagination; (2) it is an idea, a relational concept; (3) money both relies upon and creates a system of mutual trust, which derives its value from the social mechanisms maintaining that trust; (4) for money to be and remain a producer of trust, people need to have faith in it, even though the only reason to do so may be because others believe in it; (5) like mathematics and music, money facilitates communication among people even when there is no other common language; (6) it has universal convertibility; (7) when handled well, it facilities cooperation among strangers and provides a potential platform for building greater trust in one another. That is an amazingly large set of achievements.

However, as history has showed, money also creates calamities![7] Economic systems have regularly turned out to erode the very trust they rely upon to function.

The capacity to convert things from one form to another expanded greatly with the advent of credit. The core ingredient in credit was *belief*. Financiers extended credit if they *believed* it would result in a good return on investment. Or because they *believed* that in the near future people would value and pay for a potential object or service. Or because they *believed* the borrower was trustworthy. Or because they *believed* the collateral would offset the losses if the enterprise failed. However, credit would dry up during volatile periods, wars, and pestilence. During dark ages, most people lost their *faith* in the future. Lack of optimism meant fewer new businesses. That dampened economic growth. The result was less credit and even fewer businesses![8] For better and worse, *belief* and *disbelief* are fully embedded in economics' DNA.

During colonialism, most wars were financed by credit and fought by mercantile mercenaries whose sole agenda was to boost the economic strength of their businesses. Those aspirations bolstered the expansion of empires.[9] While there is a benign side of credit, the aftereffects can be very disturbing. An example is the fusion of capitalism and imperialism. Voyages of discovery were financed via credit. Finding new lands led to increased colonization. Profits from the colonial enterprises increased the wealth of the creditors. The taxes on the colonized peoples boosted the empire's resources. This led to more credit being extended to the colonies. Excessive credit exacerbated the colonies' indebtedness. Spiraling debt made the debtors more dependent on the imperial powers. And the empires grew more domineering![10]

Often people think imperial governments advanced colonization. But it was mainly the merchants who created, ran, and policed the colonies. In general, the militia created by financiers and business tycoons had more military might than the imperial nations' armed forces. An example was the mercenary army of the British East India Company that conquered the Asian subcontinent[11] and in cahoots with other enterprises made a fortune exporting drugs to China. Millions of Chinese became opium addicts. When the Chinese government tried to stop this trafficking, the negative economic impact upon the drug cartels was so severe their financiers and profiteers muscled the British government into militarily attacking China. The result was the Opium War of 1840–1842, with Great Britain being the easy victor. The subsequent peace treaty forced China to compensate the drug merchants for their financial losses caused by the Chinese government's efforts to overcome the drug-dependency problem that these foreign drug cartels had created. China was forced to give the British control of Hong Kong, so the drug lords would have a secure haven to perpetuate their Asian drug trafficking practices. The UK continued to rule Hong Kong until 1997![12]

To this day, a major part of capitalist rhetoric is the value of the free market, a rather duplicitous claim. Many people want markets free from government influence. Yet those same free-market advocates also want the freedom to pressure legislators to write laws that advance their own business profits. So, who polices these capitalists? Unable or unwilling to self-police, the uber-rich claim the government has no mandate to police them and in turn assert the right to lobby government officials on fiscal policy![13]

The field of economics has never built internal mechanisms to ensure that profits are distributed in a fair and just way. The financial world does not have within it a theory of justice. Nor does it have metrics of fairness. It also lacks the tools to assess any carnage the so-called free market leaves in the wake of the capitalist craving for an ever-enlarging economic pie.

It is worth noting that often sociotechnical innovators operated from a theological base, Isaac Newton in physics, Emanuel Kant in cosmology, and Adam Smith in economics.[14] For example, Smith, a moral philosopher who contributed considerably to capitalism's formation, used the standard religious prescriptions, namely trying to convince people to behave in specific ways, supposedly for a higher good. Capitalism proscribed what people should think, feel, and do to make economics functional. This included propagating the *belief* that economic growth is a supreme good, which releases monetary blessings that will flow down like a mighty stream![15] Smith's doctrine also held that without economic growth large profits would never be realized! And then, undoubtedly tongue in cheek, Smith, while singing the potential praises of the so-called free market, added that the whole economic system was being guided by an invisible hand![16]

There are many occasions when the moral failure of the economic system has been evident. One of the most blatant was the structure and operation of the Atlantic slave trade.

When Europeans conquered the Americas, they built an economy based on sugar, tobacco, cotton, and the mining of gold and silver, all labor-intensive ventures. Plantation and mine owners chose to maximize profits by minimizing labor costs. It was those merchants, *not the government*, who between the 16th and 19th centuries imported about 10 million African slaves. The slave trade was a supposedly free-market economic business organized in accord with the supposed laws of supply and demand! The demand for addiction-producing products like tobacco and sugar was regulated by the dynamics of freedom! How free is an addict? Demand for silver and gold existed because they had been made an essential part of the economic structure! How much freedom does a person have when forced to mine the silver and gold the coins are made of and then be paid by those very coins? The so-called free labor depended on the enslavement of innocents! How free is a slave? If one can manipulate the demand, control supply, enslave the labor, how can one characterize this as operating under a canopy called freedom?

Private slave-trading companies sold shares on the European stock exchanges. They used this money to buy ships, to hire sailors, recruit soldiers, and to purchase slaves. Then they auctioned off the slaves to local business owners. They took that cash to buy plantation products and loaded these commodities onto the ships that had transported captured slaves from Africa. Upon their return to Europe, they then peddled this merchandise at a favorable price.[17]

The so-called free-market system is not free! Calling it free is a lie! And what a devastating impact that false mirage of freedom had on the dynamics of *trust* and *belief*!

BELIEF AND BELIEBEN

It is fascinating to appreciate the role trust, faith, and belief played in the best and worst of economic times. Those three concepts, once centerpieces of philosophy, became the province of theology and religion. I think the critique of economics can be equally applied to religious dogma. Many faith traditions plucked trust, faith, and belief from the human realm and made them into emotional imperatives, which those religious institutions proceeded to dictate. People were told to have faith in God, to trust the presence of an unseen guiding hand, to believe in a loving deity or else...! The coercive quality of such practices is as oppressive as the economic elites running the world in ways that primarily advantage themselves.

The third form of decolonizing of the mind that Gandhi would ask us to make is to return trust, faith and belief to the human domain, which is where they belong. For too long they have been owned by dogma-perpetuating institutions and used as human control mechanisms, masquerading as liberating forces. Gandhi would also encourage us to recognize that we are always being supported and propped up by the abundance generated by our collective believing and collective loving. These were first given to us by nature, by those who participated in giving us life, and they are continuously offered to us by intimates, acquaintances and strangers.

I want to end this book and the topic of belief in particular with a personal message to my readers. As an educator and student of societal events, I am often asked if I am a person of faith, if I believe in God? Those are two very different questions, which need to be addressed separately. I will use my response to this query as my final words in this book on the theme of abundance.

My answer to the first question is an unequivocal *yes*. I am *a man of faith*. However, I need to sidestep momentarily what I have faith in, because at the most fundamental level, my faith has nothing to do with the divine, the transcendent, or anything metaphysical. Plain and simple, *I have faith because I am a human being*. And so does every single one of us. Having exhaustively examined my beingness, I know that probably the most familiar thing about my very existence, alongside my beating heart and my breath, is the absolute requirement to have faith.

As was discussed earlier in this book, even getting up at dawn requires faith, as does going to work, returning home, driving a car, voting, opening our hearts to others, having children, or getting married. I have faith that the sun will rise tomorrow and that the food I digest will nourish me. Put simply, I know that being a human requires faith. None of us could survive a single day without it. I have faith when scores of students and I spend long, demanding hours together in the mutual hope that the learning we jointly create will have lasting value. I have faith when I accept medical advice. I have faith that all kids in our local school will be lovingly cared for by their teachers. I have faith that if I am lost someone will help me find my way.

Every individual kneels at some altar, be it the stock market, football, the workplace, computer games, social media, the pub, rock concerts, the temple, shopping, iPhones. Every one of us is a person of faith. This is because we are people, not because we are committed to a specific faith tradition, or to atheism, nihilism, cynicism, agnosticism, or any other *ism*. We have faith because we cannot help ourselves.

When it comes to the question of whether I believe in God, obviously it is not possible for beings as small and insignificant as humans to prove if God does or does not exist, nor to establish the validity of any creed's claims. Many who are deeply committed to a belief system argue that one must have faith to know what faith is, a deeply troubling tautology, especially for those who felt they were often duped by authority figures during their youth. Faith is only faith when we doubt. So, it is understandable that people, when looking for firm ground upon which to build a life, have little interest in dwelling upon doubts, faith's essential partner!

So, do I *believe in God*? I understand that when asked this question, I am expected to address the topic of the *divine*. However, my foray into this theme ultimately led me to center on the word *believe*. Having explored to the limits of my abilities what I believed in and the many things I did not believe in, I realized that to actively not believe was as problematic as believing. Even during the times when I was sure I did not believe in something or other, I was in the inescapable *bind of believing in non-belief*. Recognizing that I, the person, was the primary agent in this, it seemed wiser to examine myself than to get fixated on the object of my potential belief or disbelief. Then I discovered that when in a state of believing I was calmer, less troubled by the world around me, more centered, more accepting of myself, less destabilized by the trivial, more embracing of others. What a surprise it was to recognize that I *believe in believing*!

What does it mean to believe? Most people think of it as a cerebral process, that to believe is to give cognitive assent to things held to be true, but for which there is inadequate evidence to support that claim. That is a misinterpretation, reinforced by how the word *belief* has come to be used in the English language, especially in this era of rationalism. In both Greek and Latin, the root of *belief* means *to give one's heart to*, where *heart* represents the deepest level of the self. This is most evident in the German word *belieben* that springs from the same source as the word *belief* in English. *Belieben* does not involve giving intellectual assent to anything. It means *to give one's heart to,* to make something the *beloved*.[18] Thus, when I say, *this is my belief* I am talking about *what I give my heart to*. This is what I make my *beloved*.

So, with that obvious freedom, I have chosen to give my heart to Love, Beauty, Truth, Peace, Authenticity, Steadfastness, Integrity, and so forth. I do this not because I know this makes sense, not because this is a rational act, not because my mind even knows how to comprehend what these words fully mean, but because I can't help myself. It is in my nature, in my humanness to give my heart, to *believe*.

And as a result of giving my heart to these things, which obviously the sages thought of as being the attributes of God, I am more connected to the universals that come from sources I cannot comprehend, that connect me with the past and the future, that draw me into a smudgy present, which includes an amorphous awareness of the transcendent quality of all existence. *Yes, I believe!* And I am surrounded by belief. My loved ones believe in me. They give their hearts to me. My world is full of believers who help support their families, their neighbors, their communities and strangers. And as they do, I am lifted and carried by the sustaining energies of others' believing actions. Plus, I believe that the cosmos believes in me. Every day it gives me the breath filling my lungs, the food that nourishes my body, the paths I elect to walk along, and a spirit that constantly reminds me of all the possibilities perpetually residing within me.

There is only one statement I can make with confidence about the theme of *God*. If we combined the total intellect of all humans over the past million years, in cosmic terms, it would be smaller than a grain of sand that existed for a nanosecond. Hence, I cannot comprehend how humanity has the hubris to express any definitive opinion about the existence or the nature of the *divine*. I know of only one resting place for those of us who are living in the universe defined by fission, fusion, gravity and electromagnetism. That is total humility. Our efforts to disassemble and reassemble life's mystery only increase its mysteriousness. I think there is very little that humanity can confidently state about what we call knowledge.

Personally, there is only one thing I know for sure. I know that *I am loved*, that *I love*, and that *love grows when given away*! If that is the only thing I have managed to figure out in this lifetime, for me, that is *more* than *enough*.

ENDNOTES

Endnotes: Introduction

[1] Allan P. Lightman, *Einstein's Dreams* (New York: Warner Books, 1994).

[2] Wikipedia, s.v. "Auguries of Innocence," last accessed 2018, https://en.wikipedia.org/wiki/Auguries_of_Innocence; William Blake's "Auguries of Innocence," a poem in *The Pickering Manuscript*, was probably written 1803 and was published 1863 in the companion volume to Alexander Gilchrist's biography of William Blake.

[3] Erik D. Olson, Diane Poling, and Gina Solomon, *Bottled Water: Pure Drink or Pure Hype?* Attachment to the NRDC Citizen Petition to the U.S. Food and Drug Administration for Improvements in FDA's Bottled Water Program (New York: Natural Resources Defense Council, Inc., 1999), www.nrdc.org/sites/default/files/bottled-water-pure-drink-or-pure-hype-report.pdf.

[4] "Top 10 Albert Camus Quotes," BrainyQuote, last accessed 2018, https://www.brainyquote.com/lists/authors/top_10_albert_camus_quotes.

[5] Kenwyn K. Smith, *MANNA in the Wilderness of AIDS: Ten Lessons in Abundance* (Cleveland, OH: Pilgrim Press, 2002).

[6] Kenwyn K. Smith and David N. Berg, *Paradoxes of Group Life: Understanding Conflict, Paralysis and Movement in Group Dynamics* (San Francisco: Jossey-Bass, 1987), 25–26.

[7] Wikipedia, s.v. "*The Limits to Growth*," last accessed 2018, https://en.wikipedia.org/wiki/The_Limits_to_Growth. Donella H. Meadows, Dennis L. Meadows, Jorgen Randers, and William W. Behrens III edited *The Limits to Growth* (1972). This report on the

computer simulation of exponential economic and population growth with a finite supply of resources was commissioned by the Club of Rome.

[8] Peter H. Diamandis and Steven Kotler, *Abundance: The Future Is Better Than You Think* (New York: Free Press, 2012), 13.

[9] Sendhil Mullainathan and Eldar Shafir, *Scarcity* (New York: Picador Press, 2013).

[10] Diamandis and Kotler, *Abundance*, 15–16.

[11] Diamandis and Kotler, 99.

[12] Diamandis and Kotler, 86–87.

[13] Diamandis and Kotler, 92.

[14] Diamandis and Kotler, 93–94; see also David Alexander, "Pentagon Weapons-Maker Finds Methods for Cheap, Clean Water," Reuters, March 13, 2013, https://www.reuters.com/article/us-usa-desalination/pentagon-weapons-maker-finds-method-for-cheap-clean-water-idUSBRE92C05720130313.

[15] Diamandis and Kotler, *Abundance*, 94–97. This is a filter of thin carbon membranes with pores about a nanometer in diameter, large enough to allow water to pass through but small enough to block molecules of salt from seawater. Because sheets of pure carbon (grapheme) are so thin (just one atom thick), it takes much less energy to push the seawater through the filter with the force required for removing salt from water. This is 500 times thinner than previous filters and 1,000 times stronger. This means the energy and pressure required to filter salt is approximately 100 times less. John Stetson, who worked on this issue, says the new filter material (Perforene), is so thin the work it takes to squeeze water through it is minimal; the membrane is thinner than the atoms it is filtering.

[16] Diamandis and Kotler, 97–98.

[17] Diamandis and Kotler, 19.

[18] Diamandis and Kotler, 40; the authors quote Matt Ridley, "Cheer Up, Life Only Gets Better," *Sunday Times*, May 16, 2010.

[19] Diamandis and Kotler, *Abundance*, 41.

[20] Diamandis and Kotler, 155–56.

[21] Diamandis and Kotler, 157. In 1986, the particle physicist Gerhard Knies of Germany determined that the world's deserts receive enough energy in a few hours to provide for humanity's power needs for a whole year. But the challenge was how to capture that energy and transport it to the large population centers.

[22] Diamandis and Kotler, *Abundance*, 172.

[23] Diamandis and Kotler, 170–171. Multiple sources are cited here: Scott Kirsner, "The Legend of Bob Metcalfe," *Wired*, November 1998; Elizabeth Corcoran, "Metcalfe's Power Law," *Forbes*, August 2, 2009; Metcalfe's Inventor Hall of Fame bio, http://invent.org/Hall_Of_Fame/353.html.

[24] Diamandis and Kotler, *Abundance*, 171.

[25] Mullainathan and Shafir, *Scarcity*, 4–10.

[26] Mullainathan and Shafir, 11.

[27] Mullainathan and Shafir, 13–15.

[28] Mullainathan and Shafir, 35–38.

[29] Mullainathan and Shafir, 20, 24.

[30] Mullainathan and Shafir, 24–29.

[31] Mullainathan and Shafir, 41–42.

[32] Mullainathan and Shafir, 63–65.

[33] Mullainathan and Shafir, 47.

[34] Mullainathan and Shafir, 65–66.

[35] David J. Chalmers, The Conscious Mind (Oxford, UK: Oxford University Press, 1996); David J. Chalmers, "Facing Up to the Problem of Consciousness," *Journal of Consciousness Studies 2*, no. 3 (1995):200–219, http://consc.net/papers/facing.html.

[36] Rollo May, *Paulus: Reminiscences of a Friendship* (New York: Harper and Row, 1973); this is a biography of the friendship Paul Tillich and Rollo May started at Union Seminary.

Endnotes: Chapter 1

[1] Ronald D. Laing, public presentation at Yale University, New Haven, CT, 1974.

[2] Kenwyn K. Smith, *Groups in Conflict: Prisons in Disguise* (Dubuque, IA: Kendall-Hunt, 1982), 7.

[3] Robert M. Pirsig, *Zen and the Art of Motorcycle Maintenance* (New York: HarperCollins,1974).

[4] Deepak Chopra, *Quantum Healing: Exploring the Frontiers of Mind/Body Medicine.* New York: Bantam Books, 1989), 225–226.

[5] Earlier, my academic pursuits included studying the underlying statistical presumptions of least-squared analysis. Realizing psychological phenomena that were five or six dimensions in character could not be understood adequately by statistics based on least-squared analysis, I started using a mathematics operating in n-1 dimensional space where "n equaled the number of relevant dimensions." This discovery led me to be cautious about accepting so-called social science findings that were many-dimensional in character but had been analyzed using only least-squared statistical procedures. See my 1970 MA thesis and my 1966 BA honors thesis.

[6] E. O. Wilson, *The Meaning of Human Existence* (London: W. W. Norton & Company, 2014), 48.

[7] Wilson, 48; see also Lawrence Anthony and Graham Spence, *The Elephant Whisperer: My Life with the Herd in the African Wild* (New York: Thomas Dunne Books, St. Martin's Griffin, 2009).

[8] Information provided by Reginal Cocroft (https//cocroft.biology.missouri.edu/people/reginald-cocroft) during Christopher Joyce and Bill McQuay, "Good Vibrations Key to Insect Communication," NPR, *Morning Edition*, Close Listening: Decoding Nature Through Sound, August 27, 2015, https://www.npr.org/2015/08/27/432934935/good-vibrations-key-to-insect-communication.

[9] Information provided by Laurel Symes, during "Good Vibrations." Key to Insect Communication," August 27, 2015, hhtp://www.npr.org/people/2100689/christopher-joyce

[10] Wilson, *The Meaning of Human Existence*, 50.

[11] Wilson, 49.

[12] Wilson, 80–81; see also Wikipedia, s.v. "Allomone," last accessed 2018, https://en.wikipedia.org/wiki/Allomone, "What Are Pheromones?" last accessed 2018, http://www.angelfire.com/ny5/pheromones5/what.html.

[13] Wilson, 83–84.

[14] Wilson, 86–88.

[15] Wikipedia, s.v. "Yin and Yang," last accessed 2018, https://en.wikipedia.org/wiki/Yin_and_yang. As an aside, how different might gender dynamics be had masculine and feminine been linked differently to charged words like *positive*, *dark*, *passive*. Although Chinese thought always made prominent both sides of any polarity.

[16] "Philosophy and Theory of Yin and Yang," Sacred Lotus Arts Traditional Chinese Medicine, last accessed 2018, http://communitymed.sbmu.ac.ir/uploads/the philosophy_of_yin_and_yang.pdf; "What Is the Yin Yang Theory?" Shen-Nong, last accessed 2018, http://www.shen-nong.com/eng/principles/whatyinyang.html.

[17] Elizabeth Reninger, "The Yin-Yang Symbol & Taoist Cosmology," *Mandala Madness* (blog), March 9, 2008, http://mandalamadness.blogspot.com/2008/03/yin-yang-symbol-taoist-cosmology.html.

[18] Alfred Huang (trans.), *The Complete I CHING* (Rochester, NY: Inner Traditions, 2010).

[19] "Philosophy and Theory of Yin and Yang."

[20] "Philosophy and Theory of Yin and Yang."

[21] Noam Chomsky, *Syntactic Structures* (Berlin: Walter de Gruyter CmbH & Co., 1957, 2002).

[22] Magoroh Maruyama, "Toward a Cultural Symbiosis," in *Evolution and Consciousness: Human Systems in Transition*, ed. Eric Jantsch and Conrad H. Waddington (Reading, MA: Addison-Wesley Publishing Company, 1975), 198–206.

[23] David Bohm, *Quantum Theory* (Englewood Cliffs, NJ: Prentice-Hall, 1951); David Bohm, *Wholeness and the Implicate Order* (London: Routledge and Kegan,1980).

[24] Ilya Prigogine, "Order through Fluctuation," in *Evolution and Consciousness*, ed. Jantsch and Waddington, 93–98.
[25] A. Tustin, "Feedback," *Scientific American*, 187 (1952): 48–55.
[26] Kenwyn H. Smith, "Rabbits, Lynxes and Organizational Transitions," in *New Futures: The Challenges of Managing Corporate Transitions*, ed. John Kimberly and Robert E. Quinn (Homewood, IL: Dow Jones-Irwin, 1982), 267–94.
[27] Prigogine, "Order though Fluctuation," in *Evolution and Consciousness*, ed. Jantsch and Waddington, 93–126.
[28] University of Alberta professor Stan Boutin and his international colleagues L. A. Wauters, A. G. McAdam, M. M. Humphries, G. Tosi, and A. A. Dhondt published an article, "Anticipatory Reproduction and Population in Seed Predators," *Science* 314 (December 2006), 1928–30, as reported in the CBC News Technology and Science section, December 2006, http://www.cbc.ca/news/technology/squirrels-time-litters-to-anticipate-food-booms-1.604047.

Endnotes: Chapter 2

[1] Inside this declaration is a self-referential conundrum: the senses scanning the universe and the mind synthesizing data gathered from and about the universe are elements of the universe itself! Intellectual enigmas like this will be addressed later.
[2] Jeanne Fowler and Shifu Keith Ewers, *T'ai Chi Ch'üin: Harmonizing Taoist Belief and Practice* (Brighton, UK: Sussex Academic Press, 2005), 5.
[3] Robert G. Henricks, "Introduction," in *Te Tao Ching*, Lau-Tzu (New York: Ballantine Books, 1989), xi; Herrlee G. Crell, *What Is Taoism? And Other Studies in Chinese History* (Chicago: University of Chicago Press, 1970), 2.
[4] Crell, *What is Taoism?* 1–24. This offers a significant commentary on the real authorship and when various bits of texts were potentially written. This is interesting material about both history and textual analytics but is not overly relevant to our

purposes here. Hence, I will refer to *Lao-Tzu* as if he is a single author, while acknowledging that this may well be a simplification that serious students of *Taoism* should not overlook. One feature of these early writings was their spacious quality, which made it possible for them to be interpreted and translated in various and even contradictory ways, which led to inevitable schisms in those identifying themselves as *Taoists* across the centuries. A solid, cryptic historical treatise can also be found in Thomas Cleary, *The Essential TAO* (New York: HarperOne, 1993,) 123–30.

[5] Henricks, "Introduction," xx–xxi.

[6] Lau-Tzu, *Tao Te Ching* #6 (Steven Mitchell, trans.) (New York: HarperCollins Publishers, 1988).

Endnotes: Chapter 3

[1] See Kenwyn K. Smith *Yearning for Home in Troubled Times* (Cleveland, OH: Pilgrim Press, 2003), 164–174.

[2] Mark Cartwright, *Yin and Yang, a Definition*, 2012, http://www.ancient.eu/Yin_and_Yang/.

[3] See Stephen Hawking and Leonard Mlodinow, *The Grand Design* (New York: Bantam Books, 2010); Max Tegmark, *Our Mathematical Universe: My Quest for the Ultimate Nature of Reality* (New York: Alfred A. Knopf, 2014).

[4] Laurence G. Boldt, *The Tao of Abundance: Eight Ancient Principles for Abundant Living* (New York: Penguin, 1999), 27–29, 31–35; Lau-Tzu, *Tao Te Ching* #1 (Steven Mitchell, trans.) (New York: HarperCollins Publishers, 1988), discussed by Boldt on p. 35.

[5] Thomas Merton, *The Way of Chung Tzu* (New York: New Directions, 1965), 40, cited in Boldt, *The Tao of Abundance,* 33.

[6] Boldt, *The Tao of Abundance*, 22.

[7] See "How Quickly Do Different Cells in the Body Replace Themselves," Cell Biology by the Numbers, last accessed 2018, http://book.bionumbers.org/how-quickly-do-different-cells-in-the-body-replace-themselves/.

[8] See Benjamin Radford, "Does the Human Body Really Replace Itself Every 7 Years?" *Live Science*, April 4, 2011, http://www.livescience.com/33179-does-human-body-replace-cells-seven-years.html.

[9] See "How Many Cells Are in the Human Body—And How Many Microbes?" *National Geographic*, January 13, 2106, http://news.nationalgeographic.com/2016/01/160111-microbiome-estimate-count-ratio-human-health-science/.

[10] See Chopra, *Quantum Healing*; Deepak Chopra, *Ageless Body, Timeless Mind* (New York: Harmony Books, 1993); Andrew Weil, *Spontaneous Healing* (New York: Alfred Knopf, 1995); Bill Moyers, *Healing and the Mind* (New York: Doubleday, 1993).

[11] Ray Kurzweil and Terry Grossman, *Fantastic Voyage: Live Long Enough to Live Forever* (New York: Rodale Press, 2004), 2–7.

[12] MedlinePlus, s.v. "Autoimmune Disorders," last accessed 2018, https://medlineplus.gov/ency/article/000816.htm.

[13] Fowler and Ewers, *T'ai Chi Ch'üin*, 57–58.

[14] Lau-Tzu, *Tao Te Ching* #29 (Steven Mitchell, trans.) (New York: HarperCollins Publishers, 1988), last stanza.

[15] Fowler and Ewers, *T'ai Chi Ch'üin*, 59–60.

[16] Fowler and Ewers, 84–85, 146.

[17] Fowler and Ewers, 151, 160–161.

[18] Fowler and Ewers, 159.

[19] Lau-Tzu, *Tao Te Ching* last portion of #48 (Gia-Fu Feng and Jane English, trans.) (New York: Random House, 1972).

[20] *The Metaphysical Functionality of the Kidneys*, Humanity Healing Network, 2011, cited in http://humanityhealing.net/2011/10/the-metaphysical-functionality-of-the-kidneys-i/.

[21] These deaths are recounted in chapter ten of Smith, *Yearning for Home in Troubled Times*, 164–173.

Endnotes: Chapter 4

[1] Jean-Francois Revel and Matthew Ricard, *The Monk and the Philosopher: A Father and Son Discuss the Meaning of Life* (New York: Schocken Books, 1999), 162.

[2] Revel and Ricard, 166.

[3] Alexander Leaf, "Every Day Is a Gift When You Are Over 100," *National Geographic* (1973): 95–118; companion document by Alexander Leaf (1973): 45–53.

[4] Alexander Leaf, "Long-Lived Populations: Extreme Old Age," *Journal of the American Geriatrics Society,* 30, no. 8 (1982): 485–487.

[5] Alexander Leaf, *Youth in Old Age* (New York: McGraw-Hill, 1975).

[6] See B. Egolf, J. Lasker, S. Wolf, and L. Potvin, "The Roseto Effect: A 50-Year Comparison of Mortality Rates." *American Journal of Public Health* 82, no. 8 (August 1992): 1089–92, https://en.wikipedia.org/wiki/Roseto_effect; Francis Weller, *The Wild Edge of Sorrow* (Berkley, CA: North Atlantic Books, 2015), 13–14.

[7] Lawrence LeShan, *Cancer as a Turning Point: A Handbook for People, Their Families and Health Professionals*, rev. ed. (New York: Plume Penguin, 1994).

[8] Salman Kahn unintentionally set off a reformation in children's education in 2004/5 when he began offering educational support to children struggling with schooling. He worked with them remotely, sending short videos of an animated digital chalkboard, which augmented lessons on standard classroom topics. Wikipedia, s.v. "Kahn Academy," last accessed 2018, en.wikipedia.org/wiki/Kahn_Academy; Diamandis and Kotler, *Abundance*, 184–186.

[9] This initial venture was undertaken by a physicist, Sugata Mitra, who was concerned about the plight of children living in Indian slums. These findings were successfully replicated in other parts of the world. See Diamandis and Kotler, *Abundance*, 174–175.

[10] Diamandis and Kotler, 176.
[11] Diamandis and Kotler, 181.
[12] Wikipedia, s.v. "Waldorf Education," last accessed 2018, en.wikipedia.org/wiki/Waldorf_Education; Wikipedia, s.v. "Montessori Education," last accessed 2018, en.wikipedia.org/wiki/Montessori_Education. The first Waldorf School was founded in 1919; a century later it was operating 1,000 schools and 2,000 kindergartens in 60 nations. Likewise, the Montessori movement, begun in 1907, has 30,000 schools worldwide, educating children, ages 2 to 18.
[13] Michael Carrithers, *BUDDHA: A Very Short Introduction* (Oxford, UK: Oxford University Press, 1983, 1996), 2–3, 12.
[14] Carrithers, *BUDDHA*, 3; Philip Wogaman, *What Christians Can Learn from Other Religions* (Louisville, KY: Westminster John Knox Press, 2014), 63.
[15] Carrithers, *BUDDHA*, 6–8.
[16] Carrithers, *BUDDHA*, 9–10.
[17] Carrithers, *BUDDHA*, 14–18.
[18] Carrithers, *BUDDHA*, 18–20.
[19] Thich Nhat Hanh, *Peace Is Every Step: The Path of Mindfulness in Everyday Life* (New York: Bantam, 1992), 95–98; Thich Nhat Hanh, *The Heart of the Buddha's Teaching: Transforming Suffering into Peace, Joy, and Liberation* (New York: Broadway Books, 1998).

Endnotes: Chapter 5

[1] Hermann Hesse (Hilda Rosner, trans.), *Siddhartha* (New York: New Directions Books, 1951), 83.
[2] Sudhir Kakar and Katarina Kakar, *The Indians: Portrait of a People* (New Delhi, India Penguin Books, 2007), 181; Fritjof Capra, *The Tao of Physics* (New York: Bantam Books, 1975), 78.
[3] *Bhagavad Gita*, 8.3, cited in Capra, 37–39 and 78.
[4] See *Encyclopedia Britannica*, 11th ed., vol. 15, 679–80: "Karma meaning deed or action; in addition, it also has philosophical and

technical meaning, denoting a person's deeds as determining his future lot;" Robert Ellwood and Gregory Alles, *The Encyclopedia of World Religions*, "Karma: Sanskrit word meaning action and the consequences of action," 253; Hans Torwesten, *Vedanta: Heart of Hinduism* (New York: Grove Press, 1994, 97); Wikipedia, s.v. "Karma," last accessed 2018. "In the Vedas the word karma applies to work, deed or action, and its resulting effect…," https://en.wikipedia.org/wiki/Karma.

[5] See Bruce R. Reichenbach, "The Law of Karma and the Principle of Causation," *Philosophy East and West* 38, no. 4 (October 1988): 399–410; James McDermott, "Karma and Rebirth in Early Buddhism," in *Karma and Rebirth in Classical Indian Traditions*, ed. Wendy D. O'Flaherty (Berkeley: University of California Press, 1980), 165–92; Padmanabh Jaini, "Karma and the Problem of Rebirth in Jainism," in *Karma and Rebirth*, ed. O'Flaherty, 217–39; Ludo Rocher, "Karma and Rebirth in the Dharmasastras," in *Karma and Rebirth*, ed. O'Flaherty, 61–89, cited in Wikipedia, s.v. "Karma."

[6] See Wilhelm Halbfass, on Karma and Rebirth (Indian Conceptions) in Encyclopedia of Philosophy (London: Routledge, 1998), cited in Wikipedia, s.v. "Karma."

[7] Deng Ming-Dao, *365 Tao Daily Meditations* (New York: HarperOne, HaperCollins, 1992), 62; Capra, *The Tao of Physics*, 37–39 and 79.

[8] James Lochtefeld, *The Illustrated Encyclopedia of Hinduism*, vol. 2 (New York: Rosen Publishing, 2002), 589, cited in Wikipedia, s.v. "Karma."

[9] Kakar and Kakar, *The Indians*, 194–96.

[10] Here are several meanings of *dharma*: "To hold, maintain and keep," see J. A. B. van Buitenen, "Dharma and Moksa," *Philosophy East and West* 7, no. 1/2 (1957): 33–40; James Fitzgerald, "Dharma and Its Translation in the Mahabharata," *Journal of Indian Philosophy* 32, no. 5 (2004): 671–85, cited in Wikipedia. Another meaning for the word *dharma* is "the established, the firm, a supporter or bearer," see Terence P. Day,

The Conception of Punishment in Early Indian Literature (Ontario, Canada: Wilfrid Laurier University Press, 1982), 42–45, cited in Wikipedia. Also the word *dharma* can mean "the rules governing the universe, the regulating of change by not regulating change, a principle preserving constancy."
[11] Steven Rosen, *Essential Hinduism* (Santa Barbara, CA: Praeger, 2006), 34, cited in Wikipedia, s.v. "Dharma."
[12] *The Concise Oxford Dictionary of World Religions* (1997), cited in Wikipedia, s.v. "Dharma."
[13] Kshiti Mohan Sen, *Hinduism* (Harmondsworth, UK: Penguin Books, 1961), 39–40, cited in Amartya Sen, *The Argumentative Indian* (London, UK: Penguin Books, 2005), 46.
[14] Kakar and Kakar, *The Indians*, 187.
[15] See Gavin Flood, "Making Moral Decisions," in *Themes and Issues in Hinduism*, ed. Paul Bowen (New York: Bloomsbury Academic, 1998), 30–54 and 151–52; H. Coward, "Hindu Bioethics for the Twenty-First Century," *The Journal of the American Medical Association* 291, no. 22 (2004): 2759–60; van Buitenen, "Dharma and Moksa," 37.
[16] Ramachandra Guha, *Gandhi Before India* (New York: Alfred A. Knopf, 2014), 200.
[17] Kakar and Kakar, *The Indians*, 188–193.
[18] Kakar and Kakar, 203.

Endnotes: Chapter 6

[1] See Smith, *Yearning for Home*.
[2] This is an idea expressed in Hermann Hesse (Rika Lesser, trans.), *Siddhartha* (New York: Barnes and Noble Classics, 2007), 113, although these are my words, not his.
[3] This American Indian image was the basis of the poem "Lost," by David Wagoner, first published in David Whyte, *The House of Belonging* (Langley, WA: Many Rivers Press, 1997).
[4] Robert A. Johnson, *Balancing Heaven and Earth: A Memoir of Visions, Dreams and Realizations* (San Francisco: Harper, 1998),

264–265.

[5] Thomas Cahill, *The Gifts of the Jews: How a Tribe of Desert Nomads Changed the Way Everyone Thinks and Feels* (New York: Nan A. Talese/Anchor Books, 1998), 108–109.

[6] Henricks, "Introduction," xvii.

[7] Henricks, xviii–xix, plus chapters 6 and 21.

Endnotes: Chapter 7

[1] Neil deGrasse Tyson, *Cosmos: A Spacetime Odyssey*. This is a 2014 science documentary television series, a follow-up to Carl Sagan's 1980 series *Cosmos: A Personal Voyage*. See Wikipedia, s.v. "Cosmos: A Spacetime Odyssey," last accessed, https://en.wikipedia.org/wiki/Cosmos:_A_Spacetime_Odyssey.

[2] Material previously published in Kenwyn K. Smith, "The Dance of Globalization: Learning, Thinking and Balance," in *Relatedness in the Global Economy*, ed. Edward B. Klein and Ian L. Pritchard (London: Karnac Books, 2006), 72–78; Smith, *MANNA in the Wilderness of AIDS*, 143–44.

[3] All of these measures we developed, along with the relevant research, are known as the "Queensland Test," see George E. Kearney and Donald W. McElwain, *Aboriginal Cognition: Retrospect and Prospect* (Atlantic Highlands, NJ: Humanities Press, 1976).

[4] A. Pattel Gray, ed. *Aboriginal Spirituality: Past, Present, Future* (Victoria, Australia: Harper Collins Publishers, 1996).

[5] Robert Lanza and Bob Berman, *Beyond Biocentrism: Rethinking Time, Space, Consciousness and the Illusion of Death* (Dallas: BenBella Books Inc., 2016), 201.

[6] This is a conservative estimate that most reputable scientists accept. However, in Cahill, *The Gifts of the Jews*, the author states, "Recently there was discovered in Australia what may turn out to be the earliest human art…were a series of circles engraved on a 130 foot sandstone monolith that takes us back 75,000 years," 53.

[7] Al Chung-liang Huang, *Embrace the Tiger, Return to Mountain*

(Mohab, UT: Real People Press, 1973, 1, cited in Gary Zukav, *The Dancing Wu Li Masters: An Overview of the New Physics* (New York: Bantam Books, 1979), 4–7.

[8] These characters were Heraclitus and Parmenides, respectively, see Capra, *The Tao of Physics*, 6–7.

[9] Capra, 6–7.

[10] Capra, 37.

[11] Capra, 37–39.

[12] Described by Fritjof Capra, *The Turning Point: Science, Society and the Rising Culture* (New York: Bantam Books, 1983), 76–77; discussed at length in the introduction of Margaret J. Wheatley *Leadership and the New Science: Learning about Leadership from an Orderly Universe* (San Francisco: Berrett-Kohler Publishers, Inc., 1994).

[13] Max Tegmark, *Our Mathematical Universe: My Quest for the Ultimate Nature of Reality* (New York: Alfred A. Knopf, 2014), 158 (including the footnote) and 160. The numbers 1 through 82 indicates how many protons an atom has (e.g., hydrogen 1 through lead 82, etc.); two atoms, technetium (43) and promethium (61), are radioactive and unstable; many atoms have more than one stable version, corresponding to different numbers of neutrons (so-called isotopes); the total number of known stable isotopes is 257. See also Wikipedia, s.v. "List of Elements by Stability of Isotopes," last accessed 2018, https://en.wikipedia.org/wiki/List_of_elements_by_stability_of_iso topes.

[14] Tegmark, *Our Mathematical Universe*, 159.

[15] Tegmark, *Our Mathematical Universe*, 159.

[16] "Slamming two hydrogen molecules (each with a pair of hydrogen atoms) together at 50 kilometers per second can break them apart so their atoms get separated…(whereas) you'd need to crash two helium nuclei (each consisting of two protons and two neutrons) at…36,000 kilometers per second" to break "them apart into separate neutrons and protons…," Tegmark, *Our Mathematical Universe*, 160.

[17] Tegmark, *Our Mathematical Universe*, 159.
[18] See Wikipedia, s.v. "List of Elements by Stability of Isotopes."
[19] *The Feynman Lectures on Physics*, passage quoted in Tegmark, *Our Mathematical Universe*, 11.
[20] Tegmark, *Our Mathematical Universe*, 160.
[21] Tegmark, 161–162; It is presumed that electrons are indivisible, having resisted particle colliding forces as strong as 99.999999999 percent of the speed of light. *Quarks* have been classified as *up quarks* and *down quarks*, with a proton having *two ups* and *one down*, and a neutron *two downs* and *one up*. The process of intense particle collisions has revealed the existence of many more-miniature sub-units, which rapidly decay into "more familiar stuff." They have been given names such as pions, kaons, sigmas, omegas, muons, tauons, W-bosons, Z-bosons. Several of these are made up of *quarks* and other newly established, unstable particles called *strange, charm, bottom,* and *top*.
[22] Tegmark, 162.
[23] Tegmark, 162.
[24] Tegmark, 162.
[25] Tegmark, 163.
[26] Tegmark, 163.
[27] Eknath Easwaran, *1000 Names of Vishnu* (Delhi, India: JAIOC Publishing House, 1997), 33–34.
[28] See Robert Lanza, "Biocentrism Builds on Quantum Physics by Putting Life into the Equation" in *A New Theory of the Universe* (2007), 11, see materials in chapter 5 discussed in Stephen Hawking and Leonard Mlodinow, *The Grand Design* (New York: Bantam Books, 2010), 75–83.
[29] Tegmark, *Our Mathematical Universe*, 45–46, 53.
[30] Tegmark, 47–49 and 67.
[31] Tegmark, 24.
[32] Tegmark, 4.
[33] Tegmark, 49.
[34] Tegmark, 49.
[35] Tegmark, 53 and 63.

[36] Tegmark, 50.

[37] Tegmark, 64.

[38] Tegmark, 69.

[39] See "Dark Matter vs. Dark Energy," published by HETEX and cited in http://hetdex.org/dark_energy/dark_matter.php.

[40] See "Dark Matter vs. Dark Energy," published by HETEX and cited in http://hetdex.org/dark_energy/dark_matter.php.

[41] Tegmark, *Our Mathematical Universe*, 70.

[42] Tegmark, 76, 87; "Dark Matter and Dark Energy," *National Geographic*, last accessed 2018, http://science.nationalgeographic.com/science/space/dark-matter/.

[43] See "Dark Matter vs. Dark Energy."

[44] Rather than recount our conversation in the casual terms we were using, I have chosen to use materials that are published and readily accessible to anyone. Most of this is beautifully presented in the work of Neil deGrasse Tyson, *Cosmos: A Spacetime Odyssey* (2014). I also draw on the well-known book from a much earlier era by Fritjof Capra, *The Tao of Physics* (1975).

[45] This idea permeates Gandhi's writings. A place where this is easily seen is in his reflections on the *Gita*, especially chapter 12 of Mohandas Gandhi, *The Bhagavad Gita: According to Gandhi* (New Delhi, India: Orient Publishing, 2011).

[46] Easwaran, *1000 Names of Vishnu.*

[47] Easwaran, stanza 1, 295.

[48] Easwaran, stanza 8, 296, and stanza 21, 299.

[49] Easwaran, stanza 10, 297.

[50] Easwaran, stanza 17, 298.

[51] Easwaran, stanza 5, 296.

[52] Easwaran, final stanza, 312.

[53] Easwaran, stanza 106, 312, and stanza 95, 310.

[54] Easwaran, final stanza, 312.

[55] Easwaran, stanza 47, 303, and stanza 44, 302.

[56] Easwaran, stanza 104, 312.

[57] Easwaran, stanza 32, 300.

[58] Easwaran, stanza 87, 309.

[59] Easwaran, stanza 5, 296.

[60] Easwaran, stanza 14, 297.

[61] Easwaran, stanza 14, 297.

[62] Easwaran, stanza 33, 300.

[63] Easwaran, stanza 71, 306.

[64] Easwaran, stanza 35, 301.

[65] Easwaran, stanza 29, 300.

[66] Easwaran, stanza 35, 301.

[67] Easwaran, stanza 102, 311.

[68] Easwaran, stanza 51, 303.

[69] Easwaran, stanza 66, 306.

[70] Easwaran, final stanza, 312.

[71] Easwaran, stanza 93, 310.

[72] Easwaran, stanza 64, 305.

[73] Easwaran, stanza 1, 295.

[74] Easwaran, stanza 18, 298.

[75] Easwaran, stanza 60, 305.

[76] Easwaran, stanza 3, 296.

[77] Easwaran, stanza 44, 302.

[78] Easwaran, stanza 18, 298.

[79] Easwaran, stanza 23, 299.

[80] Easwaran, stanza 9, 297, and stanza 19, 298, and stanza 26, 299.

[81] Easwaran, stanza 60, 305.

[82] Easwaran, stanza 12, 297.

[83] Easwaran, stanza 75, 307.

[84] Easwaran, stanza 62, 305.

[85] Easwaran, stanza 86, 309.

[86] Easwaran, stanza 13, 297.

[87] Easwaran, stanza 77, 307.

[88] Easwaran, stanza 77, 307.

[89] Easwaran, stanza 46, 303.

[90] Easwaran, stanza 6, 296, and stanza 12, 297, and stanza 27, 300.

[91] Easwaran, stanza 90, 309.

[92] Easwaran, stanza 7, 296.

[93] Easwaran, stanza 97, 310.

[94] Easwaran, stanza 78, 308.
[95] Easwaran, stanza 90, 309.
[96] Easwaran, stanza 44, 302.
[97] Easwaran, stanza 5, 296.
[98] Easwaran, stanza 96, 310.
[99] Easwaran, stanza 1, 295.
[100] Easwaran, stanza 103, 311.
[101] Easwaran, stanza 11, 297.
[102] Easwaran, stanza 45, 302.
[103] Easwaran, stanza 22, 299.
[104] Easwaran, stanza 7, 296.
[105] Easwaran, stanza 7, 296.
[106] Easwaran, stanza 42, 302.
[107] Easwaran, stanza 41, 302.
[108] Easwaran, stanza 31, 300.
[109] Easwaran, stanza 22, 299.
[110] Easwaran, stanza 41, 302.
[111] Easwaran, stanza 2, 295.
[112] Easwaran, stanza 5, 296.
[113] Easwaran, stanza 11, 297.
[114] Easwaran, stanza 21, 299.
[115] Easwaran, stanza 79, 308.
[116] Easwaran, stanza 6, 296.
[117] Easwaran, stanza 15, 298.
[118] Easwaran, stanza 51, 303.

Endnotes: Chapter 8

[1] Paul Tillich, *The Courage to Be* (New Haven, CT: Yale University Press, 1952).
[2] Smith, *Groups in Conflict*, 92.
[3] Hawking and Mlodinow, *The Grand Design*, 63–83; Lanza, *A New Theory of the Universe*; Lanza and Berman, *Beyond Biocentrism*.
[4] Hawking and Mlodinow, *The Grand Design*, 63–83; Lanza, *A*

New Theory of the Universe; Lanza and Berman, *Beyond Biocentrism*; see also Rupert Sheldrake, *Morphic Resonance: The Nature of Formative Causation* (Rochester, VT: Park Street Press, 2009).

[5] The conventional belief had long been that Aboriginal peoples arrived in Australia about 50,000 years ago. But an archeological study reported in the July 2017 issue of Nature, and reported upon by BBC News on July 20, 2017, titled "Australia Human History 'Rewritten by Rock Find,'" http://www.bbc.com/news/world-australia-40651473, indicates that the First Peoples had been in Northern Australia 65,000 years ago.

[6] Myles Gough, "Aboriginal Legends Reveal Ancient Secrets to Science," BBC News, May 19, 2015, http://www.bbc.com/news/world-australia-32701311.

[7] Gough, "Aboriginal Legends Reveal Ancient Secrets to Science," reported by Les Bursill, an anthropologist and member of Sydney's Dharawal people.

[8] Gough, "Aboriginal Legends Reveal Ancient Secrets to Science," reported by Duane Hamacher, an astrophysicist at the University of New South Wales.

[9] Gough, "Aboriginal Legends Reveal Ancient Secrets to Science." This Northern Territory site, discovered in the 1930s with the help of Luritja guides, is now the Henbury Meteorites Conservation Reserve.

[10] Gough, "Aboriginal Legends Reveal Ancient Secrets to Science," reported by Duane Hamacher about the findings of Nick Reid, a linguistics expert from the University of New England, and coauthored with marine geographer Patrick Nunn from the University of the Sunshine Coast; both are Australian universities.

[11] This is discussed fully by Lanza and Berman in their writings on biocentrism. See Robert Lanza and Bob Berman, *Biocentrism: How Life and Consciousness Are the Keys to Understanding the True Nature of the Universe* (Dallas: BenBella Books Inc., 2009); Lanza and Berman, *Beyond Biocentrism*.

[12] This is discussed fully by Lanza and Berman in their writings on

biocentrism. See Robert Lanza and Bob Berman, *Biocentrism: How Life and Consciousness Are the Keys to Understanding the True Nature of the Universe*; Lanza and Berman, *Beyond Biocentrism.*
[13] As per the discussions of *Tao*, *YHWH*, discussed earlier in this book.
[14] Yuval Noah Harari, *Sapiens: A Brief History of Humankind* (New York: Harper, 2015), 397–414.
[15] Harari, 397.
[16] Harari, 401–402.
[17] Harari, 404.
[18] Harari, 407.
[19] Harari, 409–414.
[20] Harari, 412–413.
[21] Hanh, *The Heart of the Buddha's Teaching*, 6, 9–11.
[22] Hanh, 21.
[23] Hanh, 29.

Endnotes: Chapter 9

[1] This retreat is called a *Power Laboratory*. See Barry Oshry, *Leading Systems: Lessons from the Power Lab* (San Francisco: Berrett-Kohler, 1999); Smith, *Groups in Conflict*; Smith, *Yearning for Home in Troubled Times.*
[2] Wikipedia, s.v. "Electricity," last accessed 2018, www.en.wikipedia.org/wiki/Electricity.
[3] Kenwyn K. Smith, "Toward a Conception of Organizational Currents," *Group and Organization Studies* 9, no. 2 (1984): 285–312; Kenwyn K. Smith, "The Movement of Conflict in Organizations: The Joint Dynamics of Splitting and Triangulation," *Administrative Science Quarterly* 34, no. 1 (1989): 1–20.
[4] R. Coase and N. Wang, *How China Became Capitalist* (New York: Palgrave Macmillan, 2012).
[5] For a full explication of this, see Smith and Berg, *Paradoxes of Group Life*, 46–61; Anthony Wilden, *System and Structure*

(London: Tavistock Publishing Ltd., 1972), 155–190.

[6] Gregory Bateson's discussion on "difference that makes a difference." See Kenwyn K. Smith, "Philosophical Problems in Thinking about Organizational Change," in *Change in Organizations*, Paul S. Goodman and Associates (San Francisco: Jossey-Bass, 1982), 334–45.

[7] H. C. Cooley, *Human Nature and the Social Order* (New York: Scribner, 1922).

[8] For a more expansive explication of social comparisons, see Smith, *Groups in Conflict*, 4–16 and 83–98.

[9] Stephen Mitchell (trans.), *The Bhagavad Gita* (New York: Three Rivers Press, 2000), 23.

[10] Capra, *The Tao of Physics*, 77–78.

[11] Mohandas Gandhi, *The Bhagavad Gita: According to Gandhi* (Delhi, India: Orient Press, 2011), 13.

[12] Gandhi, 29.

[13] Capra, *The Tao of Physics*, 75–77.

[14] Mitchell, *The Bhagavad Gita*; Gandhi, *The Bhagavad Gita*, 22.

[15] Gandhi, *The Bhagavad Gita*, 254.

[16] Gandhi, 34.

[17] Mitchell, *The Bhagavad Gita*, 14–18, 43; Gandhi, *The Bhagavad Gita*, 22–23.

[18] Mitchell, 43–47; Gandhi, 21, 25–27.

[19] Gandhi, 29–32.

[20] Mitchell, *The Bhagavad Gita*, 47–51, from chapter 2, stanzas 11–14, 17–20, 22, 24–25, 28, 30; Gandhi, *The Bhagavad Gita*, 34–40.

[21] Gandhi, 47.

[22] Eknath Easwaran, *Gandhi the Man: How One Man Changed Himself to Change the World* (Ahmedabad, India: Jaico Publishing, 1997), 133.

[23] Easwaran, 125–26.

[24] Mitchell, *The Bhagavad Gita*, 55, chapter 2, stanza 52.

Endnotes: Chapter 10

[1] The first time this term appeared in print was by journalist Ann Ewing in her article "Black Holes in Space," January 18, 1964, reporting on a meeting of the American Association for the Advancement of Science. John Wheeler then used it in 1967. That placed it in common use. In 1783, John Michell had speculated about a body so massive that even light could not escape, and Pierre-Simon Laplace (1796) expressed the same idea in the first two editions of his book *Exposition du Système du Monde*, see C. C. Gillispie, *Pierre-Simon Laplace, 1749–1827: A Life in Exact Science* (Princeton, NJ: Princeton University Press, 2000), 175. Also see W. Israel, "Dark Stars: The Evolution of an Idea," in *300 Years of Gravitation*, S.W. Hawking and W. Israel (Cambridge, UK: Cambridge University Press, 1989). This idea was largely ignored until Albert Einstein (1915) and Karl Schwarzschild's solution to Einstein's field equations.

[2] This paraphrases the essence reported in articles in *National Geographic* and *NASSA Science* on black holes. They are Michael Finkel, "Star Eater," *National Geographic*, March 2014, https://www.nationalgeographic.com/magazine/2014/03/black-holes-einstein-star-eaters/, and "Black Holes," *NASSA Science*, 2017, https://science.nasa.gov/astrophysics/focus-areas/black-holes, and "What Is a Black Hole," https://www.nasa.gov/audience/forstudents/k-4/stories/nasa-knows/what-is-a-black-hole-k4.html, and Nola Taylor Reed, "Black Holes: Facts, Theory & Definition," https://www.space.com/15421-black-holes-facts-formation-discovery-sdcmp.html.

[3] Where there is no chance of escaping a black hole's clutches is an imaginary zone called the *event horizon*. See D. Finkelstein, "Past-Future Asymmetry of the Gravitational Field of a Point Particle," *Physical Review* 110, no. 4 (1958): 965–967, where he gave the name event horizon to what had previously been called the Schwarzschild surface, "a perfect unidirectional membrane: causal

influences can cross it in only one direction." The event horizon is spherical for static, nonrotating holes and slightly oblate for spinning ones. See Stephen Hawking and G. F. R Ellis, *Large Scale Structure of Spacetime* (Cambridge, UK: Cambridge University Press, 1973); Sean M. Carroll, *Spacetime and Geometry* (Wooster, MA: Addison Wesley, 2004), 217–22. Outside a rotating black hole's event horizon is a region called an *ergosphere*, where objects gyrate in the same direction, but nearing the horizon, they go into reverse; to remain stationary, they must go faster than the speed of light. See R. J. Nemiroff, "Visual Distortions Near a Neutron Star and Black Hole," *American Journal of Physics* 61, no. 7 (1993): 619.

[4] See Finkelstein, "Past-Future Asymmetry," 965–967.

[5] Nemiroff, "Visual Distortions," 619.

[6] Scientists describe a black hole in terms of three independent variables, mass, angular momentum, and electric charge. For full explanations, see things like the Kerr-Newman metric, M. Heusler, "Stationary Black Holes: Uniqueness and Beyond," *Living Reviews in Relativity* 1, no. 6 (1998), doi:10.12942/Irr-1998-6 (archived from the original on 1999-02-03 and retrieved 2011-02-08). When objects enter a black hole, any information about the shape of the object or distribution of charge on it is evenly distributed along the event horizon, which is lost to outside observers. At the horizon, we have a dissipative system, which is different from other field systems that are time-reversible, like electromagnetism. The gravitational and electric fields of a black hole give very little information about what went in. The information that is lost includes every quantity that cannot be measured far away from the black hole horizon. This is called the black hole information paradox. See Warren G. Anderson, *The Black Hole Information Loss Problem. Usenet Physics FAQ* (1996), retrieved 2009-03-24; Preskill (1994-10-21) *Black Holes and Information: A Crisis in Quantum Physics* (PDF), Caltech Theory Seminar.

[7] A black hole sucking in everything in its surroundings is only correct near a black hole's horizon; far away, the external

gravitational field is identical to that of any other body of the same mass. See Michael A. Seeds and Dana E. Bachman, *Perspectives on Astronomy* (Independence, KY: Cengage Learning, 2007), 167.

[8] See G. Hooft, "The Holographic Principle," in *Basics and Highlights in Fundamental Physics*, A. Zichichi, Subnuclear series 37, World Scientific (2001), arXiv:hep-th/0003004.
See also G. Hooft, "Introduction to the Theory of Black Holes" (PDF), Institute for Theoretical Physics/Spinoza Institute (2009), 47–48.

[9] See Robert Lanza, "A New Theory of the Universe: Biocentrism Builds on Quantum Physics by Putting Life into the Equation," *American Scholar,* 00030937, vol. 76, is. 2 (2007); Lanza and Berman, *Beyond Biocentrism.*

[10] See the adult development literature for an explanation of these life transitions, especially Daniel Levinson, Charlotte N. Darrow, Edward B. Klein, Maria H. Levinson, and Braxton McKee, *The Seasons of a Man's Life* (New York: Ballantine Books, 1978); and Daniel J. Levinson and Judy D. Levinson *The Seasons of a Woman's Life* (New York: Ballantine Books, 1996).

[11] For a brief discussion of Bertrand Russell's concept of Logical Types, see Gregory Bateson, *Mind and Nature: A Necessary Unity* (New York: Bantam, 1979), 21 and 251.

[12] There is a full discussion of the character of self-reference and negation in Smith and Berg, *Paradoxes of Group Life*, 50–61.

[13] Smith and Berg, 52–53.

[14] Smith and Berg, 53.

[15] Harari, *Sapiens*, 396.

[16] Cahill, *The Gifts of the Jews*, 51–90.

[17] Cahill, *The Gifts of the Jews*, chapter 1, 11–50, especially the "Epic of Gilgamesh"; Harari, *Sapiens*, 40–62.

[18] For full accounts, see the book of Genesis in the Bible; Cahill, *The Gifts of the Jews*, 51–90; Bruce Feiler, *Abraham: A Journey to the Heart of Three Faiths* (New York: William Morrow, 2002).

[19] Feiler, *Abraham*, 40.

[20] Feiler, 62.

[21] Feiler, 43.

[22] Cahill, *The Gifts of the Jews*, 94.

[23] This is an idea suggested by Paul Tillich when he titled one of his books *On the Boundary* (New York: Charles Scribner's Sons, 1966).

[24] Feiler, *Abraham*, 45 and 60.

[25] Feiler, 49.

[26] Feiler, 47.

[27] Feiler, 52.

[28] Feiler, 63.

[29] Feiler, 63.

[30] Reinhold Niebuhr, cited on pages 169–170 of Cahill, *The Gifts of the Jews*.

Endnotes: Conclusion

[1] See H. de Soto, *The Mystery of Capital: Why Capitalism Triumphs in the West and Fails everywhere Else* (New York: Basic Books, 2000).

[2] Harari, *Sapiens*, 174–78.

[3] Harari, 179.

[4] Harari, 180.

[5] Harari, 181–185.

[6] Harari, 305.

[7] Harari, 185–187.

[8] Harari, 307–310.

[9] Harari, 316.

[10] Harari, 317.

[11] Harari, 325.

[12] Harari, 326.

[13] Harari, 328–329.

[14] Rupert Sheldrake, *The Presence of the Past: Morphic Resonance and the Memory of Nature* (Rochester, VT: Park Street Press, 2012), 56 (re Kant); Jaroslav Pelikan, *Jesus through the Centuries: His Place in the History of Culture* (New Haven CT: Yale

University Press, 1985) (re Newton); Adam Smith, *The Wealth of Nations* (New York: Barnes and Noble Publishing, 1776); Mark Skousen, *The Big Three in Economics: Adam Smith, Karl Marx and John Maynard Keynes* (New York: Routledge, 2015).

[15] The Bible: Amos 5.42

[16] Harari, *Sapiens*, 314.

[17] Harari, 329–331.

[18] Marcus J. Borg, *Meeting Jesus Again for the First Time* (San Francisco: Harper, 1994), 137; Wilfred Cantwell Smith, *Faith and Belief* (Princeton, NJ: Princeton University Press, 1979), 105–127.

CPSIA information can be obtained
at www.ICGtesting.com
Printed in the USA
BVHW071951010419
544303BV00001B/31/P